"Know your culture and unleash its power. That's the lesson that Shane Green conveys in his powerful new book *Culture Hacker*. Not only practical, but a good read, too."
—**John Baldoni, internationally acclaimed leadership educator, executive coach, and author of more than a dozen books on leadership, including MOXIE: *The Secret to Bold and Gutsy Leadership*.**

"Shane Green understands at a deep level what moves employees and cultures to greatness. *Culture Hacker* will help leaders navigate the complexities of performance, engagement and brand in a values-based framework."
—**Linda Fisher Thornton, CEO of Leading in Context and author of 7 *Lenses: Learning the* Principles and *Practices of Ethical Leadership***

"Tackling a topic like this can be daunting. The author provides fresh ideas to concepts we've all encountered in the workplace. He inspires the reader to apply his methods to improve employee engagement and retention and expand upon the development of exceptional customer relations."
—**Ed Wallace, bestselling author of *The Relationship Engine***

"Culture trumps strategy. So yes, it matters a lot. And what is culture but a collection of habits? This exciting book draws on hard-won experience to offer smart, subtle and exact ways to make your organization a better place to work, and a place that works better."
—**Michael Bungay Stanier, author of the *Wall Street Journal* bestseller *The Coaching Habit***

"Shane Green's book, *Culture Hacker*, speaks to and highlights the key component that is most critical to any organization; its culture. In a global economy, with ever changing factors constantly impacting the success and potential of any business, he provides insight and direction for the most crucial influencers to a firm's culture—it's staff. No organization, be it a bootstrapping start-up or an established successful firm can afford to ignore the valuable points he makes."
—**Anthony Melchiorri, president of Argeo Hospitality and executive producer of Travel Channel's** *Hotel Impossible* **and** *Five Star Secrets*

"*Culture Hacker* is a refreshing look at next gen HR and how to achieve a transformed work experience in your business with Shane's visionary take on change for an agile and engaged workforce"
—**Anne Fulton, founder of Fuel50 and author of *The Career Engagement Game***

"Shane sets out the most critical principle of organizational success—that engaged employees equal engaged customers. This book is critical in reminding leaders of this imperative as, despite all the evidence that employee engagement delivers not only great customer service but wider success, few organizations are making it happen day to day. Shane sets out some simple principles and actions that any leader or organization can benefit from—not just the retail or service world where the 'happy employees equal happy customers' has long been a mantra. They apply to any organization doing anything anywhere – delivering engagement through inspirational leadership must be the key objective for the successful 21st century leader.
—**Chris Roebuck, professor and author of *Lead to Succeed***

"Shane provides proof of what I've said for years: 'If you get the culture right, everything else in your business will be easier.' Even better, he gives us specific actions to take along with unique and effective methods to implement. Read *Culture Hacker* for increased sales and profits."

—**Jack Daly, Amazon bestselling author of** *The Sales Playbook*

"Company culture, whether for a startup or a Fortune 500, is the most defensible and differentiating asset you can create. It defines your potential to innovate, grow, compete, and succeed. Shane offers a clear and concise roadmap for business leaders to design and deliver an employee experience that educates and engages people to strive to deliver exceptional service. It's an important read."

—**John Gengarella, CEO, Netpulse**

"Shane Green has always been the go-to source for making company culture a strategic tool for success. With *Culture Hacker*, he opens up his playbook. A must read for anyone building a new or managing an existing company."

—**Rehan Choudrey, founder and CEO of A Beautiful Perspective**

CULTURE
HACKER

Reprogramming Your Employee
Experience to Improve **Customer Service**,
Retention, and **Performance**

CULTURE HACKER

SHANE GREEN

WILEY

Cover design: Wiley
Cover images: survey © baona/Getty Images, jumping man © bubaone/Getty Images

Published by John Wiley & Sons, Inc., Hoboken, New Jersey.
Published simultaneously in Canada.

For general information about our other products and services, please contact our Customer Care Department within the United States at (800) 762–2974, outside the United States at (317) 572–3993 or fax (317) 572–4002.

Wiley publishes in a variety of print and electronic formats and by print-on-demand. Some material included with standard print versions of this book may not be included in e-books or in print-on-demand. If this book refers to media such as a CD or DVD that is not included in the version you purchased, you may download this material at http://booksupport.wiley.com. For more information about Wiley products, visit www.wiley.com.

ISBN 978-1-119-40572-6 (cloth)
ISBN 978-1-119-40575-7 (ePDF)
ISBN 978-1-119-40577-1 (ePub)

Printed in the United States of America

10 9 8 7 6 5 4 3 2 1

I am dedicating this book to Sandra, Jagar, and Cass.

Contents

Introduction

The Journey from Customer Experience to Employee Experience

It is good to have an end to journey towards; but it is the journey that matters, in the end.[1]

– Ursula K. Le Guin, American novelist

WHILE I HAVE ALWAYS THOUGHT I would write a book, my main focus these past few years has been to build a successful company that is a great partner and resource for service-oriented companies to deliver a great customer experience as well as reducing turnover and improving productivity. I also wanted to share my insights and some best practices around what we should be doing to improve corporate culture and your employees' experience. Before I get into this, let me give you a brief overview of the journey to date and why I want you to read this book.

A lot of my professional career has been involved with hotels and hospitality—operating them, managing them, or consulting for them. The biggest influence on how I operate my business today comes from my time with The Ritz-Carlton Hotel Company. The day I became a manager at the Ritz-Carlton in 1996, my boss told me that my first priority was no longer the guest but the employee. This was a hard lesson for me, and it took a while for me to understand, because up until that point, I had been entirely focused on creating the best possible guest experience. At that moment I had to shift from delivering great guest experiences to doing the same for my employees.

Making the employee experience a priority seems simple enough, yet for me initially, and I believe for many managers still today, this seems counterintuitive. After all, haven't we been told so many times that the customer is the most important person to our business? Well, let me begin with this reality for all business owners, executives, and managers—your employees are your most important asset and focus. I know we are told that we are in the customer experience economy but I believe we have already transitioned into the employee experience economy. Are you still waging a talent war? Let me tell you: the talent war is over and the talent won. If you do not start taking better care of your talent, then as company owners, executives, or managers, you will lose your best people and a lot of money.

Now this is not something new. Some of the most successful customer service organizations just happen to be the ones that take care of their staff the best. Starbucks' former CEO Howard Shultz put it perfectly when he said, "Our first priority was to take care of our people, because they were the ones responsible for communicating our passion to our customers. If we did that well, we'd accomplish our second priority, taking care of our customers."[2]

For me happy employees equals happy customers so when I experience poor customer service and become frustrated, disappointed, or angry, it would be easy to blame the employee trying to take care of me. However, I would argue that he or she is only a small part of my poor customer experience story. Because while it is the employee's bad attitude or lack of effort that is frustrating me, the real problems are the managers and organizations behind employees that accept and many times incite that attitude or lazy behavior. I become frustrated with the employee but angry at the organization and managers who have allowed this problem to happen.

A couple of years ago I did a TV show on the Travel Channel called *Resort Rescue*. What stands out to me the most were the interactions I had with members of my production company, who always wanted me to get upset and freak out on all the employees I came across delivering poor customer service—as some of my reality show peers at the time were doing. However, I refused, because, as I explained over and over again, it wasn't the employee's fault. The owners or managers were the real villains in this poor customer service story; therefore, any frustrations should be directed toward them.

You see, it is the employees' experience at work and how their managers treat them that creates the attitude they display and is responsible for the effort they exert.

Poor customer service is often the result of a poor attitude or a lack of effort from an employee, which is often the result of a poor employee experience. Over the years as I have worked with and consulted for many organizations seeking to improve their customer experience abilities, and invariably at some point we would talk about those elements of the employee experience that were failing to instill the type of mindset and attitude that their customers expected or deserved to receive. The company I founded, SGEi, has evolved from designing and delivering customer service skill training to leadership development to what is now the methodology and thinking behind the Culture Hacker concept.

As I considered, researched, and discussed what it meant to take care of employees in the workplace, it became more and more clear that if I truly wanted to impact customer service and experience, this was the way I could do it. One article early on that sparked my thinking came from *Time* magazine's Health and Wellness issue back in 2005—before everyone was really getting on the work culture bandwagon. The article noted:

> Researchers in psychology, economics, and organizational behavior have been gradually discovering that the experience of being happy at work is similar across all professions. People who love their jobs feel challenged by their work but in control of it, have bosses who make them feel appreciated, and co-workers that they like. They can find meaning in what they do.[3]

To inspire better service, we needed to focus on creating happier and more engaged employees. As Timothy R. Clark, CEO of Leader-Factor, a consulting and training organization, says, "Highly engaged employees make the customer experience. Disengaged employees break it."[4]

Now, although the employee mindset has a significant impact on customer experience, it can also influence so much more. Employees' mindsets determine how much effort they will put into their jobs and their overall performance. Effort is important regardless of the industry or job, so employee mindset and experience matter in every business. Over the years, I have implemented our training and Culture Hacker methodology in hospitality, of course, but also in sports entertainment, retail, manufacturing, the automotive industry, real estate, the airline industry, the technology sector, on cruise ships, and at malls. We have worked with companies large and small, well established and start-ups. Regardless of your focus, if you want your people to perform better, then our methodology to improve the employee experience should be a priority for you. And, of course, this is a global issue, indicated by the fact that we have worked with companies in North America, Europe, Asia, Australia, and Great Britain.

In addition, how people feel about coming to work is going to impact your ability to retain them. If they are not happy, they probably are not going to stick around for long, especially younger workers who are a lot more comfortable moving between jobs and industries than earlier generations are. The bottom line is, the main reason so many organizations fail to keep their best and brightest talent is that they do not understand or focus on how to make their people happy at work.

Now, I hear you saying "But I thought this book was all about culture." It is, because "culture" is defined as "the collective mindset and attitude of employees about what they do and who they do it for." This mindset manifests itself in *how* employees do things or, in other words, their actions and behaviors when interacting with customers, peers, and the business itself. And culture is top of mind for many owners, executives, and managers today, as indicated by a recent Bersin by Deloitte *Global Human Capital Trends* report that reads: "Employee engagement and culture issues exploded onto the scene, rising to become the number one challenge around the world in our study. An overwhelming 87% of respondents believe the issue is 'important,' with 50% citing the problem as 'very important'—double the proportion in [the previous] year's survey."[5] So there is obviously plenty of talk, but based on the continued lack of great customer service and high turnover rates, there is not enough action. Whether you like it or not, culture must be a priority in your business today.

So I came up with Culture Hacker, a methodology for improving the employee experience and mindset at work. The focus was simple and clear, with a quote from Campbell Soup CEO Douglas Conant guiding our thinking: "To win in the marketplace you must first win in the workplace."[6] I wanted to help as many organizations as possible win in the workplace so their customers could receive a better experience. Over the years I have put together a great team of customer experience and human resources experts to execute on this Culture Hacker methodology with our clients.

When I talk about culture, I often get asked "Can you really change it?" My answer is yes, because I truly believe you can affect how people think and feel. Now, you can never control a person's attitude 100% of the time, but I certainly think you can have a big impact on it. One of my favorite quotes on attitude is by Pastor Charles Swindoll, who suggests that life is 10% what happens to people and 90% how they respond to it.[7] I believe that organizations have a 90% chance of positively influencing how people feel about their jobs though the employee experience. This is an important idea, because while we might not be able to influence our employees' attitude 100% of the time, it suggests that we can certainly make a difference most of the time. And that is an important point for me. Companies can do more to make their people feel better, which in turn will ensure better customer service. And yet many businesses are not and that really frustrates me.

Companies can improve their employees' mindset or change their culture but it is generally not some easy, short-term initiative, and it cannot just be made up along the way. The process of focusing on and evolving culture can never stop, because employees are always changing. Evolving a culture is a transformational process that requires its own plan, the right resources, a focus on the right things, and, most important, the right leaders. So even once you have the right culture in place, you need to constantly measure and check the pulse of your people as their expectations and those of your customers evolve.

Although Culture Hacker is about change, I suggest that a reason we have been so successful with our methodology is that we do not make a big deal about that change. We all know that when we start talking about change, people become uncomfortable, resistant, or even antagonistic. When you start making proclamations of change, people will get scared, which will cause them to be unable to contribute to or support any positive cultural transformation. Remember that when you loudly declare change is on the way, you will also cause the militant few to gather the troops and make it their life mission to resist anything that is suggested or implemented, no matter how positive the intended outcome. So as you approach the idea of hacking or transforming your culture, do it without all the fanfare. Speak loudly with your actions, not your words—like a hacker whose work happens without the end user noticing any change, at least initially. This is the core of our Culture Hacker approach—being subtle and exact, without causing a lot of fuss or distress.

As an example of what not to do consider this example from a client I worked with. A company executive sent a video out to the entire company, stating that their culture was broken and it was time for change. Talk about adopting the completely wrong approach toward change and improving their culture. We saw an employee base that became not only frozen by the idea of change but also miserable, because they were told that their culture and, more specifically, that they as service providers were broken. Rather than promoting a large cultural change and telling everyone that the culture is off, we quietly focus in on individual mechanisms (as explained in this book) that are relatively easy to explain and manipulate, even though they are a part of a larger change effort. Simply put, Culture Hacker is about making big changes quietly.

I want to mention here in the introduction the importance of technology. Technology is changing—and, arguably, enhancing—every aspect of our lives, our jobs, and even the employee experience. New technology is changing how our staffs work, and so it is important that we recognize that the employee experience of the future and many of the mechanisms that influence our employees' mindsets will be managed and organized by technology. Today technology is prevalent in interviewing, onboarding, communication mechanisms, performance management, recognition, career development, and training. So what is the relationship between technology and culture? In their *Harvard Business Review* article, Ashley Goldsmith and Leighanne Levensaler proposed this: "[W]e like to think of values as the beating heart of culture, processed and organizational structure as the brain, and technology as the nervous system that makes sure heart and head are working together to move us forward."[8] To reiterate this idea, in each chapter we have indicated some technology companies that might be effective partners in a particular area of improving the employee experience. We recommend learning more about the many solutions out there because technology is going to be prevalent in crafting any employee experience, whether we like it or not.

Finally, let's talk about money, specifically how much you pay your employees. Although this book explains the most influential mechanisms that define how your staffers feel about coming to work, I do not spend time discussing salaries or wages. The reason is twofold. First, research indicates that money is not a strong motivator in employee performance and engagement.[9] Generally, once basic needs have been met, money is not the motivator we think it is. Second, I do not focus on salary or wages because I recognize that it is often not an easy variable to change, especially in a small business or when you are not in a position to effect salary increases. So the Culture Hacker methodology focuses on everything else that can influence the culture and mindset of employees.

Speaking of small businesses, because I have owned, coached, and managed a few of them over the years, I am very aware of the stresses and challenges associated with owning and running such ventures. As a result, I wrote this book with small business owners in mind too. The lessons and practices offered apply just as easily to small companies as to large ones. In fact, I've written this book in such a way that small business owners with limited or no human resources infrastructure can and *must* use the tactics herein to stay competitive and grow.

I wrote this book to share my insights, best practices, and inspiration for how you can create, manage, or hack your culture—to improve your customers' experiences, your employee retention, and organizational performance. By impacting all three things I know there are direct benefits to the profitability and performance of any company, which is why I believe the focus on culture should be a priority for every business person today. Thank you for reading, and thank you for wanting to make a difference in how your people feel about coming to work. There's one more nice side effect of all this—it will make *you* happier at work too!

Notes

1. Ursula K. Le Guin, *The Left Hand of Darkness* (New York, NY: Ace Books, 1987.), p. 183.

2. Howard Schultz, *Pour Your Heart Into It* (New York, NY: Hyperion, 1997), p. 182.

3. Jyoti Thottam, "Work: Thank God It's Monday!" *Time* 165, no. 3 (January 2005). http://content.time.com/time/magazine/article/0,9171,1015878,00.html

4. Timothy R. Clark, "The 5 Ways That Highly Engaged Employees Are Different," TLNT, June 19, 2012. https://www.eremedia.com/tlnt/the-5-ways-that-highly-engaged-employees-are-different/

5. *Global Human Capital Trends 2015: Leading in the New World of Work* (New York, NY: Deloitte University Press, 2015). https://www2.deloitte.com/content/dam/Deloitte/at/Documents/human-capital/hc-trends-2015.pdf

6. Quoted in Jennifer Robinson, "Saving Campbell Soup Company," *Gallup Business Journal*, February 11, 2010. http://www.gallup.com/businessjournal/125687/saving-campbell-soup-company.aspx

7. Charles R. Swindoll, "The Value of a Positive Attitude," Insight for Living Ministries (November 2015). https://www.insight.org/resources/daily-devotional/individual/the-value-of-a-positive-attitude

8. Ashley Goldsmith and Leighanne Levensaler, "Build a Great Company Culture with Help from Technology," *Harvard Business Review* (February 2016). https://hbr.org/2016/02/build-a-great-company-culture-with-help-from-technology

9. Tomas Chamorro-Premuzic, "Does Money Really Affect Motivation? A Review of the Research," *Harvard Business Review* (April 2013). https://hbr.org/2013/04/does-money-really-affect-motiv

1

Culture

More Than Just an HR Thing

Brand is just a lagging indicator of a company's culture.
—Tony Hsieh, CEO of Zappos[1]

EVERY OWNER, EXECUTIVE, AND MANAGER is responsible for his or her team, department, or company culture. No excuses. Culture is no longer just a human resources (HR) priority or thing; it is a fundamental business thing.

Culture is the collective mindset and attitude of your employees. The mindset your employees bring to work every day determines how they will take care of your customers, how much effort they will put into their work, and whether or not they will stay with you long term. The impact of a negative culture within an organization is tremendous. Poor customer interactions, high turnover, and under performing employees cost organizations—depending on their size—thousands, millions, and even billions of dollars. The research from across industries is clear: when your employees are more engaged, your company is more productive and profitable; leading to better shareholder returns. Culture is the most important business thing today.

1

When it comes to culture, the question is not "Do you have a culture?" because you do, and every company does. The real question is "What type of culture do you have today, and is it meeting the expectations of your owners, customers, and employees?" This question really is at the heart of what every manager must consider: Is your culture making your business better, delivering the desired individual and team performance, turning customers into fans, and causing your best people to stay? If it is not, know that there are things you can do to change your culture to where you and your staff want it to be.

Many owners, executives, and managers focus their energies and investments on business, financial, operational, or marketing strategies, but the reality is that a culture strategy will have a greater impact on your business than any other thing. Peter Drucker's phrase "Culture eats strategy for breakfast"[2] is probably more relevant in business today than ever before. Employees are the ones defining your business, it's value and reputation, and for that reason, the ability to attract, retain, enable, and maximize your talent is critical for your business today.

Culture is a *business* thing, and all owners, executives, and managers must be involved (along with HR, if you have that department) to get the right culture in place for your business. According to Jay Haines, founding partner of Grace Blue, a global executive search company, "The cultural piece is to my mind now the single most important component of any chief executive role."[3] Now, the problem I see in many organizations is that culture is just an HR responsibility. Whether I'm speaking with an owner, executive, or manager, when I ask who is responsible for the company's culture, the person almost overwhelmingly says "human resources." This is the first problem I have with many organizations and the people running them today—they are leaving the task and responsibility of employee attitude up to a single person or team, when, in fact, it is everyone's responsibility. As HR expert Michelle Crosby recently stated on our *Culture Hacker* podcast, "Culture needs to be owned by leaders at every level. Human resources has to play a role as a facilitator of that process, but not the owner of that process."[4] So with HR acting as the facilitator, everyone else must take on the responsibility of creating, supporting, and delivering an employee experience that instills a positive mindset, a delight in serving others, and a desire to make things happen.

Now, if you are an HR manager or, in fact, any manager who views culture as a priority, you may be nodding your head in agreement, but I bet you are also thinking about those owners, executives, or managers around you who need some convincing. So let's consider in more detail the three areas where I think culture is most strongly impacting your business's profitability and performance today: your customer experience, how much effort your people put into their work every day, and your ability to retain your best and brightest people.

How Culture Determines the Customer's Experience

As you read in the introduction, I wrote this book because of the lack of service and consideration offered to customers by so many organizations today. Obviously, I want to make sure this point is front of mind. Now, I have sat with managers who plainly told me they are not a service-based organization, so maybe these rules do not apply. My response was simple: "Do you have customers?" Their response, of course, was yes. I continued on to say that in today's world, you need to start thinking of your business as a service-based organization, no matter your product or industry, because customers, regardless of what you are providing them, expect service, a great experience, or even just appreciation in return for their business. Also, when it comes to customers, you must understand that organizations have both internal and external customers. Although some of your staff members will not deal with external customers, they work either directly or indirectly with other employees, or internal customers, who do. So when we talk about delivering a great customer experience or service, we also want to consider how staff members work with each other to deliver the products and services of the organization.

We know attitude is critical in customer interactions, both internally and externally. There is an old hospitality axiom that says "Those with a good attitude always provide great service. Those with a poor attitude always provide poor service."[5] This truth of hospitality is important in all industries, because it reminds us that the mindset and attitude of your staff members is probably the single most important aspect of making your internal or external customers feel good and of making your company successful. This line of thinking is not new. It was documented and demonstrated in the 1998 *Harvard Business Review* article "The Employee-Customer-Profit Chain at Sears," wherein the authors demonstrated that employees' attitudes led to a better customer experience and, in turn, better profits.[6]

So attitude, or how your employees feel about their jobs, defines the service and experience each customer receives. Every business owner and manager needs to be considerate of their employees' mindset when it comes to customer experience because those attitudes determine how your customers are treated, and how you treat your customers is what they talk about and share with their family, friends, and acquaintances, both in person and online. And specifically, what is being shared online is currently defining your reputation and brand more than any advertisements or marketing initiatives can do today. Mercedes-Benz CEO Steve Cannon said it best: "Customer experience is the new marketing."[7] Customer experience is being defined by how your employees feel, and it indirectly tells us a lot about how you treat your employees. As Michelle Crosby said on the podcast, "The customer experience is a reflection of what is happening inside the organization, whether the organization intends or wants it to. What you reap on the inside is what you sow on the outside."[8] What is happening inside every organization is some type of employee experience. And that experience is manifesting itself in how your employees feel about coming to work, which in turn is defining how your customer feel after every interaction.

Every interaction with your customer counts, whether to increase customer loyalty or customer spend. Lowe's Home Improvement provides compelling findings regarding the impact of employee engagement and customer satisfaction and sales. By quantifying the relationship between employee engagement and sales (starting in 2007), Lowe's found that a conservative difference between the highest- and lowest-engaged stores was more than $1 million in sales per year.[9]

We have worked with the automotive industry for a number of years, and our work with dealerships, which are either small, one-off businesses often run by a family or centers that are part of larger automotive groups, has reinforced our belief that a focus on the employee experience leads to better customer experiences and profits, due to increased market share. What is most interesting about automotive dealers is that the majority of their revenues come from servicing a vehicle, not selling it, yet many consumers view the process of taking their car in for service as not unlike going to the dentist—very painful. When car dealerships emphasize customer service in the scheduling, drop-off, pickup, and follow-up process, they delight their customers and build not only a strong, loyal customer base, reflected in repeat sales, but also a strong word-of-mouth reputation for service reliability around their community or town. And those touchpoints are all influenced and defined by the interactions customers have with and the attitudes of staff members. Your employees' mindsets definitely impact the loyalty of your customers and the financial position of your company.

Zappos CEO Tony Hsieh's quote, used to introduce this chapter, is a great line to remember. It basically says your brand is a reflection of your culture, not the other way around as most business people would have you believe. It highlights just how important culture is when it comes to a brand, and it reinforces why, for owners, executives, and managers, culture might be the most important area of focus today in terms of customer service and experience.

How Culture Determines Employee Performance

Great customer service and experience requires a lot of effort, and effort is the result of the energy someone directs toward a task. But a focus on culture is not just about better customer service; it applies to all tasks, roles, and jobs. You have to invest in your culture to ensure that your employees give their best and perform at their best.

A big part of the difference among average, good, and great is the attitude or mindset that people have. Attitude affects energy levels, cognitive ability, and how people feel. Although you cannot guarantee or expect that everyone will be positive and happy all the time, you want to ensure that you are not causing undue stress or negativity and that, for the most part, the experience of working at your company supports a positive disposition. A study by economists at the University of Warwick in England found that happiness led to a 12% spike in productivity while unhappy workers proved 10% less productive. As the economists put it, "Human happiness has large and positive casual effects on productivity. Positive emotions appear to invigorate human beings."[10]

The impact of a positive mindset cannot be downplayed in the work environment. Renowned sports psychologist Jim Taylor said:

Negative emotions can also hurt you mentally. Your emotions are telling you that, deep down, you're not confident in your ability to perform well and achieve your competitive goals. Your confidence will decline and you will have negative thoughts to go along with your negative emotions. Also, since your negative emotions are so strong, you will likely have difficulty focusing on what will help you to perform well; the negative emotions draw your attention onto all of the negative aspects of your performance. Finally, negative emotions can hurt your motivation to perform because you just don't feel good and it's no longer fun.[11]

In work as in sports, you cannot underestimate the impact of a negative attitude on performance.

One business that relies on and requires constant around-the-clock effort from employees is a cruise ship, where staff often work for weeks without time off, depending on the length of the cruise. During our time implementing a new culture within a European cruise ship company, the executive team focused on investing in the crew experience and found an improvement in effort and performance across all disciplines on the ship. When it comes to the amount of effort your employees put in each day, how they feel about their work and who they do it for matters significantly.

How Culture Determines Employee Retention

The attitude a person has about coming to work is also important in determining whether they are likely to stay with you. As full employment in many industries is coming closer to reality, employees simply have more options. What makes our current situation so interesting is that at the same time, the Millennial workforce is becoming the largest employee group. This generation and those who will come after them are more and more comfortable moving between jobs and industries to maximize their earning potential and find a greater sense of meaning in their work. That last point is critical; members of the next generation of employees will continue to leave jobs, managers, and companies that do not make them feel valued, provide purpose, or help them grow. In other words, they leave companies that do not give them a great experience.

It is also important to recognize that you are not just competing with and losing talent to those within your industry. The reality of a global economy and an informed workforce is that talent transcends most industries. The founder of the Future of Work community, Jacob Morgan, says: "We are seeing a global talent war, not only in a particular industry or location, but with employees around the world." He goes on to say, "What can an organization do to retain and keep top talent? Focus on employee experience and create an environment where employees want to show up, not necessarily where they need to show up."[12]

With workers more comfortable and willing to leave you if you do not meet their expectations, the threat of turnover is real. The costs of such turnover are striking, both to the bottom line and, psychologically, to the staff who remain. In 2016, Julie Kantor, president of Twomentor, LLC suggested that the hard costs can range anywhere from 16% to 213% of a person's salary, when you take into account training, onboarding, interview expenses, and advertising costs. Soft costs include lowered engagement for remaining employees when someone leaves, loss of productivity for new hires (it can take up to two years to reach the same level of productivity as someone who has left), impact on morale, gossip, and less effective service.[13]

One company that struggled with turnover due to a poor culture is CHG Healthcare Services. The following case study illustrates the changes that CHG made to its culture and the impact those changes had on its turnover rates.

Case Study: CHG Healthcare Services

CHG Healthcare Services is a healthcare staffing organization that serves thousands of hospitals throughout all 50 states in the U.S.[14] In an industry plagued with high turnover, between 50% and 60% per year, CHG has not only managed to retain talent, but has also become a constant fixture on some of the most sought after company recognition lists. 2016 was the company's seventh consecutive year on Fortune's "100 Best Companies to Work For" list, and eighth consecutive year on the "Training Top 125" list, to name a few. However, this success was not always the case, and the company experienced many obstacles when trying to rework their company culture.

On a recent *Culture Hacker* podcast, Kevin Ricklefs, senior vice president of Talent Management, shared that the company had over 50% turnover

(continued)

(*continued*)

15 years ago. This costly business issue was the catalyst for making a change. "When we wanted to reduce turnover, we started by asking our leaders and employees their opinion of our culture," Kevin said.[15] Giving employees a voice created a culture of feedback and a sense of ownership in the organization that is still present today. This focus on feedback positively impacted the leadership and communication style of the organization. As Kevin describes, "We give the employees every opportunity to have a voice in the company, and they continue to give us feedback and continue to help us be better."[15]

But giving employees a voice about the type of employee experience they desired was only part of the process. The real lesson here is that CHG was willing to make some tough decisions to show that they were serious about making a positive cultural shift. Some of the toughest decisions included letting go of managers who were not willing to change or support the new empowered workforce at CHG. These tough decisions are why so many companies like to talk about cultural change, but so few undertake the necessary steps to make it a reality.

While the thought of changing culture can be overwhelming, Kevin provides some advice to the brave souls undertaking the journey: don't try to go it alone. "Culture is everyone's responsibility because it is about the employee experience. We train the employees and leaders on how to build a good culture and what we mean by a good culture. This aligns everyone in the organization."[15]

For me, the best organization has an employee mindset where the experience of both internal and external customers exceeds expectations, every employee delivers his or her best, and there is below-industry turnover because the people want to be there. Quite simply, this must be the focus of every person owning or running a business today. Gallup in 2016 stated that "highly engaged work units outperformed disengaged work units by 10% in customer loyalty and engagement, 21% in profitability, and 20% in productivity."[16] The business case is clear and compelling.

Whether you are an owner, executive, manager, or HR practitioner, in today's world, culture—the current attitude of your staff—must be your most important consideration, and delivering a better employee experience must be the most important thing that you focus on. Herb Kelleher, ex-CEO and cofounder of Southwest Airlines, said it best:

"Your employees come first."[17] If you put your employees first, then their experience at work becomes your top priority. And as American author and businessman Stephen Covey said so perfectly, "The main thing is to keep the main thing the main thing."[18] For us and for every manager, executive, and owner out there, that "main thing" must be the employee experience and its impact on culture.

Culture Hack: Every owner, executive, and manager is responsible for his or her team, department, or company culture.

1. Culture is the mindset and attitudes of employees about what they do and who they do it for. This manifests itself into how effectively they work with internal and external customers.
2. Employee interactions with customers and what customers share about your business form the basis for your reputation and brand in today's transparent social media–driven world.
3. The mindset and attitude of your employees plays a significant role in how well they perform. How someone feels about coming to work affects their energy levels and even their cognitive abilities.
4. It is important for the success of your business that you retain your best and brightest over the long term by creating a great culture—a place they want to work.
5. Improving how an employee feels about coming to work requires the management and manipulation of the mechanisms that influence an employee's experience. Culture Hacker is a methodology and series of tasks that will positively impact your employee experience. It requires the engagement and support of all owners, executives, and managers.

Notes

1. Tony Hsieh, *Delivering Happiness: A Path to Profits, Passion, and Purpose* (New York, NY: Grand Central Publishing, 2010), p. 151.
2. Quoted in Shep Hyken, "Drucker Said 'Culture Eats Strategy for Breakfast' and Enterprise Rent-A-Car Proves It," *Forbes*, December 5, 2015. http://www.forbes.com/sites/shephyken/2015/12/05/drucker-said-culture-eats-strategy-for-breakfast-and-enterprise-rent-a-car-proves-it

3. Quoted in Katie Richards, "5 Tips for Building a Real and Successful Company Culture," *Adweek*, March 24, 2016. http://www.adweek .com/news/advertising-branding/5-tips-building-real-and-successful-company-culture-170383

4. *Culture Hacker* podcast, 2017. Season 1, Episode 4. On-air talent includes: Michelle Crosby, Shane Green.

5. Harry Nobles, "Attitude Can Make the Difference," *Hotel Online* (January 2001). https://www.hotel-online.com/News/PR2001_1st/Jan01_AttitudeDifference. html

6. Anthony J. Rucci, Stephen P. Kirn, and Richard T. Quinn, "The Employee-Customer-Profit Chain at Sears," *Harvard Business Review* (January–February 1998). https://hbr.org/1998/01/the-employee-customer-profit-chain-at-sears

7. Quoted in Jim Tierney, "Mercedez Benz CEO: Customer Experience Is the New Marketing." *Loyalty360* (October 2014). https://loyalty360.org/content-gallery/daily-news/mercedes-benz-ceo-customer-experience-is-the-new-marketing

8. *Culture Hacker* podcast, 2017. Season 1, Episode 4. On-air talent includes: Michelle Crosby, Shane Green.

9. Cedric T. Coco, Fiona Jamison, and Heather Black, "Connecting People Investments and Business Outcomes at Lowe's: Using Value Linkage Analytics to Link Employee Engagement to Business Performance," *People & Strategy* 34, no. 2 (2011). www.hrps.org/resource/resmgr/p_s_article_preview/ps_34.2_peopleinvestments.pdf

10. Andrew Oswald, Eugenio Proto, and Daniel Sgroi, "A New Happiness Equation: Worker+Happiness = Improved Productivity," *Warwick Economics Research Institute Bulletin* (October 2009). https://www2.warwick.ac.uk/fac/soc/economics/research/centres/eri/bulletin/2009-10-3/ops/

11. Jim Taylor, "Sports: The Power of Emotions," *Psychology Today*, December 1, 2010. https://www.psychologytoday.com/blog/the-power-prime/201012/sports-the-power-emotions

12. Jacob Morgan, "Why You Are Not Just in a War for Talent with Your Competition," *Forbes*, July 15, 2016. http://www.forbes.com/sites/jacobmorgan/2016/07/15/why-you-are-not-just-in-a-war-for-talent-with-your-competition

13. Julie Kantor, "High Turnover Costs Way More Than You Think," *Huffington Post*, February 11, 2016. http://www.huffingtonpost.com/julie-kantor/high-turnover-costs-way-more-than-you-think_b_9197238.html

14. CHG Healthcare Services, n.d. http://www.chghealthcare.com

15. *Culture Hacker* podcast, 2017. Season 1, Episode 6. On-air talent includes: Kevin Ricklefs, Shane Green.

16. Gallup, "Q12 Meta-Analysis Report," *Gallup*, 2016. http://www.gallup.com/ services/191489/q12-meta-analysis-report-2016.aspx

17. John Huey, Gordon Bethune, and Herb Kelleher, "Outlaw Flyboy CEOs Two Texas Mavericks Rant about the Wreckage of the U.S. Aviation Industry— and Reveal How They've Managed to Keep Their Companies above the Miserable Average," *Fortune*, November 13, 2000. http://archive.fortune .com/magazines/fortune/fortune_archive/2000/11/13/291563/index.htm

18. Stephen R. Covey, *The 8th Habit: From Effectiveness to Greatness* (New York, NY: Free Press, 2005), p. 160.

2

Values

Not Some Philosophical BS

Culture is a consequence of a company's values.
—Charles Day, founder of Lookingglass[1]

VALUES THAT ARE DESIGNED AND delivered clearly and consistently are critical in reprogramming your employees experience and thinking. They are the foundation of your company culture.

Let's discuss the importance of values and the fact that they are not just some "philosophical bullshit," which are the exact words some of my clients used on more than one occasion. Although values are dismissed by many managers, they might be the single most important cultural mechanism and tool that managers need to be using today if they want to get more out of their associates.

Philosophical Bullshit

Yes, I know many companies have values—they are just something you are meant to have. However, for many organizations and their managers, these values offer little—excuse the pun—value. It does not take long for me to determine if an organization's values are BS. In our

13

cultural assessments, we consider customer feedback on interactions with staff to see if the values are being adhered to. We look at employee feedback on their experiences and feelings at work to see if the values are acted on in the workplace. But even simpler, we just ask employees randomly in the organization if they have company values and, more specifically, what they are. The majority of the time we get some vague answer, even from managers, that there are values, but people are not exactly sure what they are. In one survey where we asked this question, only 8% of respondents were able to name or paraphrase what their organization's values were. So yes, for the most part, we know little importance is given to values, yet they could be the very thing that significantly improves your customer and employee experience and protects your company's reputation.

Values guide everyone in the organization on how to act and interact successfully with the customer, each other, and the company, and they guide many of the decisions, both small and large, that are made every day. Let's consider the importance of values in more detail.

Values Describe How Work Gets Done

Values are like the ground zero of a culture, or, as PepsiCo CEO Indra Nooyi said, "Values make an unsinkable ship. You cannot deliver value unless you anchor the company values."[2] They describe how things should be done while showing staff members how they can be successful within the company. They define how staff members should interact with the organization, customers, and their peers. Culture, as previously defined, is a mindset or attitude that manifests itself internally. Values—and more importantly, the behaviors associated with them —are how people demonstrate that mindset externally to those around them.

Think of values as the rules of how to work successfully with others in the company. Having values is like establishing the rules of the sandbox for young children. If those sandbox rules aren't laid out by their parents before entering the sandbox, a child can cause unintentional chaos as they play by their own set of rules. This is not unlike what is happening in many workplaces, especially when a younger workforce dominates the employee ranks. When we do not define the rules of the sandbox or rules on how work gets done, newcomers will quickly develop their own rules, upsetting the status quo and tenured staff. Does that sound familiar? By defining the rules for how things get done, we can minimize frustrations while enhancing teamwork between new and tenured staff.

In addition, values allow organizations the opportunity to do two very important things successfully: grow and replicate themselves. Remember that as a business leader, once you have worked out what you are doing and how to do it, the focus for any business is to grow, either within its current location or by replicating itself in multiple locations. The one thing that always comes with growth is the need to bring on more people. If those people, regardless of their location, are not following a set of rules that form a critical part of the business's formula for success, that business will be in trouble. Although getting the *what* right allows you to have a great company, getting the *how* right allows you to grow or replicate yourself effectively. So if you want to grow or are now growing, you better have clearly defined values in place laying out the rules of your sandbox.

Values are also critical in defining how to interact with customers. Interactions with customers are determined by how your employees feel at that moment and their subsequent behaviors, words, and actions. Values basically state the mindset that is desired and required for both internal and external customer interactions. More specifically, the behaviors attached to each value should clearly articulate for employees what they should do during those interactions. Just maybe, if we focused on promoting and reinforcing *how* work gets done, especially with our customers, there would be a heck of lot fewer poor customer interactions.

We worked with a large resort in the Caribbean that wanted to empower and encourage its front-line managers and staff to make decisions to help guests in the moment rather than constantly going to a senior manager for approval. When we rebuilt the company's values, one of those values was leadership. The idea was that regardless of their position or if they had a management title, every person was expected to exhibit leadership in all that they do. The behaviors associated with that value were to be proactive, make decisions, and inspire others with your actions. By defining the behaviors around a value that described how individuals should work, we were able to engage more staff in helping guests in the moment, as opposed to waiting for managerial approval.

Values Guide Decision Making

In addition, values guide the decision-making process at all levels of the organization, including hiring, performance ratings, knowing what to do and how to do it, and even to determine what new products or services are created.

In simple terms, a well-defined set of values directs employees and managers toward what is most important. Many years ago, we worked with a large technology organization in Silicon Valley to help its campus and services team provide better service to the thousands of campus staff. As we initially worked on developing the training curriculum, one manager approach me and candidly shared that he was not sure that focusing on the service skills of staff was the right use of their time and resources. During this conversation, I started to talk about the company's core values, specifically one that stated "Focus intently on customers," and what this meant. Although he thought it referred to only external clients and consumers, I talked about the concept of internal customers and the important role they played in the success of the company. The discovery that what we were doing was directly in line with the values and, in fact, would make this value come to life within the organization made all the difference to the buy-in of this manager and his team. The whole training program around service skills and the attitude that was needed in the various campus roles became anchored in this value, ensuring significant improvements in internal customer satisfaction and overall company performance.

Values should also guide the decisions we make with our customers every day. When we are faced with a customer challenge, request, or need and are unsure how to respond, those values and the corresponding behaviors should act as the perfect partner to allow us to make decisions and act appropriately, quickly, and efficiently. As mentioned earlier, the large Caribbean resort used its values to guide employee thinking and decision making.

On a much larger scale, consider some of the most-reported company scandals of the past couple of years; you could argue that they were created by a lack of adhering to or being guided by shared company values.

Consider the Volkswagen scandal in 2015 wherein senior executives insisted discrepancies in their emissions reports were the result of technology issues rather than intentional deceit. Without laying blame, if VW had strongly adhered to its company values of sustainable, collaborative, and responsible thinking, this would never have been a question because those values seem to be the perfect guide to help ensure such an event would never occur.[3] Unfortunately, as with many companies, when values are just a series of words found on a website or sheet of paper, they become little more than philosophical BS, which should not be the case.

One company that impressed us with the use of values to guide its decision-making process is SendGrid, discussed in the next case study.

Case Study: SendGrid

SendGrid is a leading cloud-based email service for growing companies. The organization was born out of its founders' frustration with having important messages undelivered. Isaac Saldana, Tim Jenkins, and Jose Lopez, mentored by the TechStars accelerator program, founded SendGrid in 2009.[4] Though the company started with just a handful of customers and no staff, it had a strong vision and set of unique values. Today, SendGrid employs over 300 employees across four U.S. cities and a number of supporting offices in Europe, and it is preparing for a 2017 initial public offering.[5]

One of the biggest assets that has contributed to SendGrid's unprecedented growth has always been its culture, based around their four foundational values of Honest, Happy, Humble, and Hungry. Cofounder Isaac Saldana said, "With these core values, it's easy to love coming to work every day."[6] The values have been embedded into every process within the organization, from job descriptions and hiring to performance and growth. Saldana said that using these values allows team members to "understand that the path to our goals is as important as the goals themselves."[7]

As the company has scaled, those values have been even more essential to live by. CEO Sameer Dholakia wrote in a recent interview, "A challenge as a company scales can be around creating a line of sight between what an employee does every day and the company vision . . . the

(continued)

(*continued*)
culture resonates in every person I've met at SendGrid. It isn't just words on paper."[8]

   This focus on values has truly paid off for SendGrid. In 2016, it was named to the first-ever Forbes Cloud 100 list, as one of the top private cloud companies in the world.[9] SendGrid looks to expand even further in the next few years, with plans to employ an additional 400 new hires—tripling the current employee base—by the year 2020. CMO Scott Heimes credits the company's success entirely to the team members and to the company's "4H ethos: Honest, Happy, Humble, and Hungry."[10]

The difference between companies that have values that are an integral and relevant part of their culture and a company that does not is that employees within the company with the values-based foundation have clarity, guidance, and rules around how to act and interact with others and make decisions, large or small, in both day-to-day operations and at the ownership or executive levels. The growing understanding of the importance of values is why so many companies are looking to build or rebuild their values today.

But as I said earlier, although many organizations already have values, they are nothing more than philosophical BS. Why are their values failing to provide the sort of leverage and focus I have described? Well, we find there are five main reasons that an organization's values are not having the effect they should:

1. The values have become outdated and are less relevant and meaningful to the modern worker. Although many values may be timeless, their descriptions or the behaviors associated with them just do not hold up in today's fast-paced, technology-influenced, transparent world. As a result, those values do not resonate with modern workers. Talentkeepers' 2013 Global Talent and Retention report in 2013 found that 37% of overall attrition occurs in the first year as a result of a "poor fit between the individual and organizational values."[11]

2. Employees do not realize your values even exist. To be effective, values need to be seen and utilized in many critical aspects of the

organization, such as selection, onboarding, and recognition, to name just a few.

3. There are just too many values, so employees have a hard time knowing what is most important.
4. The values are too vague—people do not know what they mean. No tangible and measurable behaviors are attached to the values, so they are open to interpretation. If values are open to interpretation, it will be hard to utilize them to select, recognize, and hold people accountable. Values must be observable, tangible, and measurable.
5. Company leadership doesn't support the values, so they become trite phrases passed down through generations. It is common to find business owners and managers who fail to communicate their actions, beliefs, and support for the organizational value.

If your values fail to provide clarity, meaning, and guidance to your people because of one of the reasons just discussed, it is time to refresh or rebuild your culture's foundation. Our work on getting your culture right begins with putting a set of simple and relevant values in place. As we have developed or reworked the values for many organizations, we have some simple yet important rules to adhere to when it comes to crafting your values.

Rules for Building or Refreshing Your Cultural Values

- Involve your staff in the process. By asking for their insights and ideas, they will feel like they have ownership and more of a responsibility to work by the values.
- Less is more. Start with a goal of crafting just four values. You can add more later. Too many values become confusing and meaningless to people.
- Give each value a short description that is easy to understand.
- Associate behaviors that are observable and measurable with each value. We usually provide three behaviors with each value.

An outcome of clearly defined values, descriptions, and behaviors may look something like Table 2.1. Note that we refer to this example throughout the book as we demonstrate how to utilize and align values and behaviors within certain cultural mechanisms.

Table 2.1   Values and Behaviors

Creative: Nothing Is Impossible	Collaborative: Contribute and Support
1. Be open to new ideas and opinions. 2. Focus on solutions. 3. Ask "Why?" and/or "Why not?"	1. Share information and ideas. 2. Follow up and follow through. 3. Listen to understand.
Accountable: Ask for Forgiveness, Not Permission	**Passionate: Love What You Do or Why Bother?**
1. Step up and make decisions. 2. Take responsibility for your actions. 3. Be transparent with your beliefs.	1. Learn something new every day. 2. Support the endeavors of your team. 3. Contribute to the growth of yourself, your team, and the organization.

Once the values are identified they need to be incorporated throughout the organization. Probably the most important step when it comes to implementing and incorporating values and behaviors is to get your managers comfortable and confident with what those values mean and why they are important—after all, they are going to be responsible for bringing those values to life and leading by example with them. How can you do this right? First, provide your managers with the reasons why your values are important. Remember, they have seen these or similar values in the past, but up until now have not really had to worry about or do anything with them. Utilize the information just provided—talk about the opportunity to grow the business, the need to have everyone working and thinking in a similar way to get things done, and the importance of having a guide for all decision making.

Next, ensure you clearly explain what each value means, how the behaviors will be observed and measured, and what is expected of each manager to bring these values to life. Educate your managers on your values well before you introduce them to the staff. It is important that managers can understand, articulate, and demonstrate the values before any staff education occurs. As an experienced trainer, I can tell you that the first thing employees do after hearing about some new value, behavior, or skill being introduced is to watch the managers to see if they are adhering to and doing what has just been taught. This observation period staff is probably the most critical part of any training or communication, because it allows staff members to understand if what they learned about is going to stick or is just another nice idea. Our work in the classroom or online is either reinforced or wasted, depending on what participants see from managers after each lesson. Get your managers ready for this moment by giving them time to absorb and practice the desired behaviors and attitudes.

Having implemented values for numerous organizations I can tell you that half of the managers will embrace your new values, while unfortunately the other half may not. As such, this next step is important when it comes to your managers. You need to make representing and promoting the values an expectation of being a manager in your organization. So often, when I look at lists of expectations of managers, I see nothing about their need to set the example for achieving the values of the company. Make this a part of their performance expectations so that all of your managers understand it is a priority and it is not going away.

The next step—and the reason you should read the rest of this book—is that you must fuse and align your values into everything you do that is central to the employee experience, from the selection process, onboarding, and informal and formal feedback to communication and leadership development. In this way, managers will know this is not some quick fix or flavor-of-the-month idea or initiative. This means they'll have to pay attention, because so many of their activities and responsibilities as managers now include these new or refreshed values. In other words, you are not giving your managers much of a choice. If they want to continue being a part of your company and want to be successful, they must become champions of your values. In a recent *Culture Hacker* podcast, Kevin Ricklefs, the senior vice president of Talent Management at CHG, gave us this key to the success of CHG's culture initiative: "We use the language of our core values throughout all we do."[12]

Invest the time to ensure your managers have every opportunity to get on board with the values and desired behaviors before introducing them to your staff. Getting your managers comfortable with the values and behaviors is the most important and subtle way to ensure that people act and interact in the right way.

When it comes time to introduce the values to your staff, consider an internal marketing campaign. Get your marketing team or person involved to develop a series of communication messages and tools that are creative and effective to introduce and reinforce these important ideals.

As we suggested, it is important to include as many employees as possible in the process of developing or rejuvenating your values. It gives them buy-in and ownership. This is also important because we believe you should review how relevant and meaningful the values are to the staff every 12 months. Bring a group of staff members together and have them share their thoughts on the values and their relevancy to their roles and responsibilities and how the company should make decisions. Don't be afraid to challenge your values to meet the changing needs of your most important constituents—your owners, your customers, and, of course, your employees. Ask for feedback and ideas about how values can be improved. The change may be as simple as adding a value (one of the benefits of starting with only a few) or modifying the descriptions or associated behaviors of another.

An example of a company engaging its people to update their values is Build-a-Bear. In 2012 they added "di-bear-sity" as one of their core values after receiving employees' input on what updates should be made.[13] The point is, don't just develop values and think they will be relevant forever. As mentioned earlier in the chapter, too many companies allow their values to become outdated. Be prepared to review and reflect on company values annually.

What does success look like when it comes to values? For me, it is when values are aligned throughout the organization with employee selection, onboarding, recognition, and accountability. Seeing the values being utilized throughout the company within all the various cultural mechanisms is critical. The values also should be promoted and talked about in meetings, memos, and be seen on screen savers and walls. Managers need to understand how to utilize, leverage, and be the example of your values and must talk easily about how each value can make a difference. And most important, your employees can talk about the company values and discuss why each one is important and what is expected of them.

Your values are not some philosophical BS or just nice ideas. If you are going to develop a better business, one that can support the growth of your company as new employees come on board, then articulating and demonstrating to everyone in your company how to act, interact, and make decisions is nonnegotiable. Your company values are the foundation of your employees' mindsets and experience with you. Invest in defining *how* your company gets work done, and make your values a part of everything you do.

Culture Hack: You must define your team or company values to be the foundation of your employees' experience.

1. Values must have clearly defined behaviors that are observable and measurable connected with them.
2. Values should be aligned and found in many other cultural mechanisms, such as the selection process, orientation, performance enablement, recognition, having tough discussions, and making tough decisions.
3. Consider refreshing your values if currently they are not a focus of your organization. Utilize the Rules for Building or Refreshing Your Cultural Values (pg. 19).
4. Allow your management team time to understand and take on the new values before introducing them to the staff. Require your managers to promote, communicate, and demonstrate your values at every opportunity.
5. Market and promote your values and their accompanying behaviors throughout the organization in all messaging, training, and meetings.

Notes

1. Quoted in Katie Richards, "5 Tips for Building a Real and Successful Company Culture," *Adweek*, March 24, 2016. http://www.adweek.com/news/advertising-branding/5-tips-building-real-and-successful-company-culture-170383
2. Quoted in PTI, "Fundamentals of India Are Strong: Indra Nooyi," *Economic Times*, November 15, 2013. http://economictimes.indiatimes.com/news/company/corporate-trends/fundamentals-of-india-are-strong-indra-nooyi/articleshow/25837245.cms

3. Volkswagen, "Our Values. Responsibility and Sustainability." *What We Stand For*. n.d. http://www.volkswagen-karriere.de/en/what_we_stand_for/our_values .html

4. SendGrid, "About Us," n.d. https://sendgrid.com/about/

5. Shabana Arora, "SendGrid to Hit $100 Million in Revenues, Plans to Be IPO Ready by 2017," *Martech Advisor*, August 19, 2016. https://www .martechadvisor.com/articles/email-marketing/martech-advisor-qa-with-scott-heimes-cmosendgrid/

6. Conor Norris, "SendGrid Co-Founder and President Isaac Saldana Talks Growth and Company Culture," *The Founder*, May 21, 2013. http://blog .founderscard.com/2013/05/21/sendgrid-co-founder-isaac-saldana-talks-growth-and-company-culture/

7. SendGrid, "Our Founders" n.d. Quote attributed to Isaac Saldana. https:// sendgrid.com/careers/

8. Jillian Wohlfarth, "A Q&A with Sameer Dholakia, SendGrid's CEO," SendGrid, December 4, 2014. https://sendgrid.com/blog/interview-with-sameer-dholakia-sendgrids-ceo/

9. David Friedman, "SendGrid Named to First-Ever Forbes 2016 World's Best 100 Cloud Companies List," *PR Newswire*, September 8, 2016. http://www .prnewswire.com/news-releases/sendgrid-named-to-first-ever-forbes-2016-worlds-best-100-cloud-companies-list-300324584.html

10. Chloe Aiello, "SendGrid Will Hire as Many as 250 by Early 2018, Close to 400 by 2020," *Denverite*, November 28, 2016. http://www.denverite.com/ sendgrid-will-hire-many-250-early-2018-close-400-2020-23753/

11. Quoted in Career Engagement Group, "Hold on Tight—Retention Is Now the Issue: An In-Depth Look at Engagement and Retention in Changing Economic Times," white paper by Career Engagement Group (April 2014), p. 11.

12. *Culture Hacker* podcast, 2017. Season 1, Episode 6. On-air talent includes: Kevin Ricklefs, Shane Green.

13. Holly Lebowitz Rossi, "7 Core Values Statements That Inspire." *Fortune*, March 13, 2013. http://fortune.com/2015/03/13/company-slogans/

3

Selection

The Right Fit over a Warm Body

Many companies don't have an engagement issue; they have a hiring issue.
—Bob Kelleher, thought leader[1]

FOR THE HEALTH OF YOUR organization and sanity of your people it is critical to select new people into your organization that are a cultural fit just as much as they are a job fit.

It's time to talk about selection. One of the most important roles a leader has is selecting the right people to be a part of the team. Although his work is controversial, a quote from Italian philosopher Niccolò Machiavelli is appropriate to mention here: "The first method for estimating the intelligence of a ruler is to look at the men he has around him."[2] This is a powerful idea for any manager: how would you be judged if I looked at the people you hired?

We all know that selecting the right person is important. Plenty of research suggests that hiring the wrong person will result in lost productivity, increased turnover, and increasingly disengaged staff. Most important, merely putting a warm body in front of your customers will harm your reputation and brand very quickly. It will also frustrate every single one of your current employees who have to deal with the wrong person. The dispositions of the people you hire says a lot about what you think about your other staff members and yourself. Yet many managers focus on getting someone to fill a role as quickly as possible without any consideration for the person's cultural fit.

And that is often the situation in which we find most companies. When we talk to managers, they are focused on getting people to complete tasks. When it comes to fit, managers are, first and foremost, focused on the person's ability to complete a task. Managers may say they consider organizational fit, but most simply consider whether they like the person. Often managers hire more for a fit with themselves than with their company. So let's consider how to improve the selection process to help align individual values with the organization's values so that new hires are set up for success from the very beginning.

Begin with Job Fit but Shift Quickly to Cultural Fit

When looking to hire someone, managers have to begin with a job match or fit, ensuring candidates have the skills, dispositions, and intelligence to complete the tasks required. Some positions require more emphasis on skills than others. Once the basic requirements have been met, managers must emphasize culture fit. "Job fit" means candidates have the skills, expertise, and experience to do a job, while "culture fit" means they adhere to a set of values and have a personality and disposition that is aligned with how things get done within your organization. In today's modern world, culture fit is as important as job fit. And I would argue that in most service-oriented positions, you can teach the necessary skills and behaviors, but you can't teach the character to be great with customers. Patrick O'Connell is the owner and a chef of The Inn at Little Washington; he is consistently recognized as one of America's best restaurateurs. As O'Connell pointed out, "We found over time that nice people can be taught almost anything."[3]

Late LA Lakers owner Jerry Buss stated, "Everybody can see the skillful players, but the question is, 'Are you willing to wait until you find a skillful player with high character?' because eventually, the character is what wins out on the court."[4] This is a great reminder about how to build a winning team. It is easy to find people with skills and industry experience, but what managers really want to find is a person with skills and experience who also has character. It might take a little longer to find that person, but it is the character that will contribute most to the performance of a team in the long term.

How can managers ensure they select someone with the right experience and skill set as well as the personality and mindset to be successful in the organization? To select the right person, not just another warm body, managers must use behavior-based questions and activities, get other associates involved in the interview process, and perform a thorough reference check. Let's consider each of these steps in more detail.

Use Behavioral Interview Questions

Behavioral questions, where you focus in on past experiences is an effective way to determine job fit as well as cultural fit. As mentioned earlier, one of the most important reasons to have clearly defined values is that they make a great guide for managers when they are selecting people to be a part of the team because they focus in on cultural fit. Mark Zuckerberg, CEO of Facebook, is a proponent of this method for his own company. He said, "In terms of attracting people, I think one of the most important things is just being upfront about what you stand for. Facebook is not a company for everyone."[5] I want to reiterate this important point for you: Not everyone who puts in an application deserves to work for you. It is not because they are bad people, it's just that at this particular moment, they do not have the mindset, qualities, or values to help your organization or the people in it get better.

What are behavioral questions, and how can companies create their own? Behavioral interviewing is a style of interviewing that was designed by industrial psychologists in the 1970s. The philosophy behind this interview style is that one of the best ways to predict future performance is to review past performance in similar situations.[6] During the interview process, interviewers ask a series of questions about past experiences and behaviors that line up with current company values. To capture the previous experiences of an applicant, interviewers might consider questions with phrases such as:

- Describe a situation in which you . . .
- Tell me about a time when you . . .
- Give me a specific example of a time when you . . .
- What is your typical way of . . .

- Compare and contrast the times when you . . .
- In your most recent role . . .
- Over the course of your career . . .

To aid in understanding, we have developed some behavioral questions from the values developed and described in Chapter 2 (see Table 3.1).

Remember that the questions developed for culture fit are also very supportive of, and useful in, helping you determine the job fit, so be sure to use behavior-based questions to confirm an applicant has the right job skills and experience. A large automotive manufacturer we worked with provided its dealerships with a series of behavioral questions designed to help find people who were good cultural fits with the brand. Although that was one of the outcomes, various dealership managers found that these questions actually allowed them to find people well suited for the job too. Job fit and cultural fit are not mutually exclusive, and both support the idea of finding the right person for the job.

Also, during the interview process, consider asking potential candidates about their ideal job, work environment, or boss. These simple questions can provide great insight into how candidates might fit into the current role and the things that will impact their success. It is surprising how many times interviewees will describe their ideal job or work and it will be very different from what you are offering. People have been trained to give "ideal" answers to many typical questions. By asking them to define *their* perfect job, they speak to their true selves and often provide your clearest insight into who they really are.

Don't forget that during any interview, the interviewer must be open minded and aware of biases. Biases are a natural part of being human and may include stereotyping gender, age, religion, or race. In addition to being aware of your own personal biases, I suggest involving others, especially staff members, in the interview process.

Use Group Interviews

One of the best interview practices is to involve a few members of staff in a speed interviewing process not unlike a speed dating experience, where people sit together for five minutes or less in quick conversations. We used this type of interview successfully within The Ritz-Carlton

Table 3.1 Example of Behavioral Questions to Determine Culture Fit

Creative: Nothing Is Impossible

1. **Be open to new ideas and opinions.**
   "Tell me about a time when you were open to new ideas and the opinions of others."
2. **Focus on solutions.**
   "Give me a specific example of when you focused on solutions."
3. **Ask "Why?" and/or "Why not?"**
   "Please describe an important assignment or policy where you asked 'Why?' or 'Why not?'"

Collaborative: Contribute and Support

1. **Share information and ideas.**
   "How do you typically share information and ideas with others? Please describe a specific example."
2. **Follow up and follow through.**
   "Tell me about a recent project or assignment when you followed through with your commitment to another person or team."
3. **Listen to understand.**
   "Give an example of when you listened to someone to understand his objective."

Accountable: Ask for Forgiveness, Not Permission

1. **Step up and make decisions.**
   "Tell me about a time when you had to step up and make a decision."
2. **Take responsibility for your actions.**
   "Give me a specific example from your most recent job of how you took responsibility for your actions."
3. **Be transparent with your beliefs.**
   "In your career, tell me about a situation in which you were the most transparent with your beliefs? What was the outcome?"

Passionate: Love What You Do or Why Bother?

1. **Learn something new every day.**
   "What did you learn yesterday?"
2. **Support the endeavors of your team.**
   "Tell me about a time when you supported the efforts of your team members. How did you contribute to their success?"
3. **Contribute to the growth of yourself, your team, and the organization.**
   "In the last year, how did you contribute to the growth of yourself, your team, and/or the organization?"

Hotel Company. As a manager, I was introduced to this method as a way to find candidates who responded well under pressure. As it was explained to me, if a job candidate is still smiling 30 minutes after being interviewed and bombarded with multiple questions from multiple people, then he or she probably can smile when bombarded by all our guests. I have never forgotten this lesson and still recommend the speed interviewing process to my clients. Also, by arming staff with a couple of questions and having them involved in the process, you can help ensure that any possible first impression biases are minimized during the interview process. An additional benefit is that once a candidate is hired, the staff members who were part of the interviewing process have some interest in making the new hire successful—after all, they helped in making the decision to bring that person on.

Also remember that potential candidates are interviewing the brand too. Candidates today are much more conscious of their fit with an organization, as they recognize this is a key aspect of their experience and ability to grow. This is another reason why speed interviewing with multiple staff members is a great idea, because they are the ones completing the work and can describe the benefits and challenges of the role accurately. According to Ron Fry, the author of *101 Smart Questions to Ask on Your Interview*, the question of a new employee's fit is central to the interviewer's thought process.[7]

To ensure an effective group or team interview process, I recommend creating a simple scorecard that every interviewer is responsible for completing after the interview. Interviewers should provide a score from 1 to 5 for job fit and culture fit. They should also provide any notes that they think are important to consider when making the final decision. Figure 3.1 is the scorecard we use; consider it an example. Using a scorecard is a best practice utilized by companies that want to make the selection process a priority and that understand the importance of getting the right people on board.

Add an Activity-Based Component to the Interview

Another best practice we have seen and support is to place candidates into a situation, setting, or exercise where they are asked to complete a task either individually or as part of a team. The purpose of these exercises is to see firsthand a candidate's personality traits and

Interviewer: Date:			
Candidate Name and Position	Job Fit Score	Culture Fit Score	Notes
Note: Scores on 1–5 scale. 1 = not; 5 = completely			

Figure 3.1   Interview Scorecard

responses when faced with a challenge. One of our favorite examples is from Lego, a company that places a lot of emphasis on culture fit during the job interview and loves to implement activity-based interviews. See the following business case.

Case Study: LEGO

With an iconic brand and over 13,000 employees worldwide, LEGO continues to be a leader in the toy market. However, it hasn't always been that way. LEGO's lack of focus led to a decline in sales, placing the company near bankruptcy by 2003.[8] Moreover, an increase in digital toys and games decreased the popularity of LEGO products. The company reestablished their

(continued)

(*continued*)

focus on the core business and devised an action plan to regain success. Re-focusing on their values and mission helped align employees and redirect the company. While there are many important culture lessons in regards to LEGO, this case focuses on the emphasis they place on employee selection. When it comes to hiring, LEGO utilizes a unique yet thorough interview process to select the candidates that best fit their culture. The selection process is meant to assess an individual's creativity, passion, and ability to have fun, as these are important virtues for any employee to be successful at LEGO.[9] LEGO's values of imagination, creativity, fun, learning, and caring, serve as a guide to select employees. LEGO strives to hire employees who are authentic, and whose personal values fit with the organization.[9] Kimberly Burton, Human Resources (HR) manager for LEGO Australia and New Zealand, explains, "Focusing on the job description isn't enough. We include the values and brand framework of our company as a foundation to our job interviews."[10] Individuals' values and characteristics are discovered during the interview process by asking specific questions and utilizing activities that relate to the company's values. For example, candidates are asked to build something with LEGO bricks that represents themselves. Through this process, interviewers can also assess the applicants' fun and imagination with the products. LEGO's HR Director, Jennifer Langone, recalls, "Watching future employees build a part of themselves is very memorable and reflective of our spirit and values."[9]

By spending time on selecting for cultural fit, LEGO is able to align employees' efforts and retain talent more effectively. While their selection process is an important aspect of continuing LEGO's strong culture, it is also integral to their business success and expansion plans.

Complete Those Reference Checks

In addition to interviewing carefully, it is important to complete reference checks. They are an important reinforcement of the perceptions and perspectives gained in the interview process. Although managers may learn only limited information, they will be able to confirm titles, dates, and tasks. If the reference is comfortable sharing more information, managers can focus on the candidate's strengths and accomplishments. Also, managers should take a moment to review a candidate's LinkedIn profile for insights on character.

See some suggestions for completing a reference check in the following box.

Reference Check Reminders

- Try to speak with the direct supervisor/manager of the candidate to ascertain both their job and culture fit.
- Ask job fit questions to ascertain title, employment dates, and job tasks. Ask the reference to describe the responsibilities and tasks completed.
- Ask culture fit questions to determine the typical behaviors and attitudes of the candidate. Utilize a couple of your culture fit behavioral questions when possible.
- Ask about a candidate's strengths and greatest accomplishments while in the role. If possible, you might be able to ask about their weaknesses, also.

Finally, remember that the experiences potential candidates have during their interview process need to be memorable. Even if they might not be the next employees, they could be new customers for the brand. Provide a professional, respectful, and memorable interviewing process by: offering an interviewee a warm welcome and a form of gratitude for coming into interview; ensuring interviewers are prepared, are on time, and are ready to answer questions if asked; and offering interviewees a break and a beverage if they are meeting multiple people and will be with the team for more than an hour and a half. Always remember to thank the interviewee again as they depart and clarify when they can expect to hear from you.

Ensuring a great interview process is another area of the employee experience that technology can help. A number of software solutions help both interviewers and interviewees to better understand each other, share important information about the interview, and allow a more streamlined approach to managing all the information about an applicant both before and after an interview. Some examples include Cornerstone Recruiting, Oracle Taleo Recruiting, IBM Kenexa Brass-Ring, and Great Hires. As Ray Tenenbaum, the founder of Great Hires, a candidate experience software company, recently told us on the

Culture Hacker podcast, platforms like Great Hires "are increasing the transparency in the hiring process, enhancing the company's reputation for those selected and even those that aren't."[11]

Do not forget about the post-interview process. After the interview, remember to be professional by following up as expected, giving updates as required, and notifying candidates one way or another as soon as a decision is made. It is a nice touch if, after the interview, regardless of whether the person is selected or not, the team sends each interviewee a thank-you note or message. Remember the interview process is an opportunity to showcase your brand's culture and values and enhance your reputation, so put your best foot forward. The candidates might not become employees, but they can still be customers or impact how others think about your company.

Listen, I get it; with all the pressures managers deal with to get the job done and take care of customers, there is always a wish to just get someone into a role. However, of all the things we seem to be doing quicker in this modern economy, team selection is the one area where I suggest slowing down. You may not get every hire right, but by utilizing behavioral interview questions, involving other employees in the interview process, implementing an activity or exercise, and performing a thorough reference check, you give yourself the best possible chance to get the best person for the job and your organization. I cannot reiterate enough how important it is to select carefully. As Robert Mellwig, senior vice president of Really Cool People at Two Roads Hospitality, a hotel management company, said, "You have to ensure that the cultural connection trumps all else when hiring and retaining the right employees."[12] The success of your teams and your culture depends on it.

Culture Hack: Select new employees who are a cultural fit as much as a job fit.

1. Begin with a job match or fit, ensuring candidates have the skills, disposition, and intelligence to complete the tasks required. Once these requirements are met, cultural fit is necessary for an employee's long-term success.
2. Create and use behavioral interview questions centered around your values. Create and use a behavioral scorecard when interviewing candidates to rate their cultural fit.
3. Involve staff members in the interview process to get multiple insights into an applicant's cultural fit and to enhance the buy-in once the new person comes on board.
4. Use a situation, setting, or exercise where applicants complete a task or role-play, either individually or as part of a team, to gain insights into their personalities, dispositions, and skills.
5. Always do your due diligence when hiring employees by conducting reference checks.

Notes

1. Bob Kelleher, "10 Practical Employee Engagement Practices," *Business NH Magazine* (June 2015). http://millyardcommunications.com/index.php?src=news&refno=5277&category=News
2. Erika Andersen, "15 Surprisingly Great Leadership Quotes from Machiavelli," *Forbes*, July 31, 2014. http://www.forbes.com/sites/erikaandersen/2014/07/31/15-surprisingly-great-leadership-quotes-from-macchiavelli/
3. Tahl Raz, "A Recipe for Perfection." *Inc.*, July 1, 2003. http://www.inc.com/magazine/20030701/25658.html
4. Quoted in Kevin Ding, "As Draft Draws Near, Lakers Appear Destined to find Jahlil Okafor an Ideal Pick," Bleacher Report, June 9, 2015. http://bleacherreport.com/articles/2490870-as-draft-draws-near-lakers-appear-destined-to-find-jahlil-okafor-an-ideal-fit
5. Mark Zuckerberg, "The Facebook Founder in His Own Words," *Fortune* (December 2016): 72. http://fortune.com/facebook-mark-zuckerberg-business/

6. Faith Bliga, "Behavioral Interviewing vs. Traditional Interviewing," *Applicant Stack*, May 23, 2011. https://www.applicantstack.com/blog/2011/behavioral-interviewing-vs-traditional-interviewing

7. Nicole Fallon Taylor, "10 Insightful Company Culture Questions to Ask Your Interviewer, *Business News Daily*, March 17, 2016. http://www.businessnewsdaily.com/8897-company-culture-questions.html

8. Richard Feloni, "How Lego Came Back from the Brink of Bankruptcy," *Business Insider*, February 10, 2014. http://www.businessinsider.com/how-lego-made-a-huge-turnaround-2014-2

9. Heather Wood Rudulph, "How to Get Hired at LEGO," *Cosmopolitan Magazine*, June 11, 2015. http://www.cosmopolitan.com/career/interviews/a41715/interview-insider-lego-career-jobs/

10. Craig Donaldson, "LEGO's 5 Keys for Improving Cultural Fit," *Inside HR*, January 15, 2014. http://www.insidehr.com.au/legos-5-keys-for-improving-cultural-fit/

11. *Culture Hacker* podcast, 2017. Season 1, Episode 2. On-air talent includes: Ray Tenenbaum, Shane Green.

12. *Culture Hacker* podcast, 2017. Season 1, Episode 1. On-air talent includes: Robert Mellwig, Shane Green.

4

Orientation and Onboarding

Your Sink-or-Swim Strategy Is a Terrible Waste of Talent

A good first impression can work wonders.

—*J. K. Rowling, author*[1]

ONCE YOU HAVE DECIDED TO hire a person to join your organization, the next step in the process is to orient and onboard them. It is important that any new staff members connect emotionally with the organization and are set up for success in their first 30 days. Unfortunately this is often not the case. As a result, I believe the orientation and onboarding process is one of the most poorly managed and under-delivered cultural mechanisms for many organizations.

If you are really serious about setting your staff up for success and ensuring they have the right attitude and mindset to be successful from the beginning, you cannot continue to ignore the orientation and onboarding of your new people. We see organizations invest heavily in getting the right people hired and then fail to introduce, immerse, and train them correctly. Consider how staff members start their new jobs with you and whether or not you set them up for success. Do you do anything to connect them emotionally to your brand? Do you introduce them to your values or show them how to be successful with you? Do you have an organized and systematic approach to getting people trained in an environment where learning can happen and mistakes made? Unfortunately, most of the companies we begin working with answer no to most of these questions. As a result, they answer yes to the question "Is the high turnover of first year employees the direct result of them deciding in the first couple of days that this will only be a short-term stop due to you making a horrible first impression?"

A poor beginning is not just a front-line issue; it happens throughout all levels of an organization, executives included. The lack of an inspiring and effective orientation and onboarding process and program causes many selection decisions to be based more on experience and skills than on culture fit. This means that rather than orienting and onboarding new employees correctly and effectively, managers can get their new hires working right away, throwing them into their new roles and seeing if they sink or swim, fail or succeed. After all, that is what they used to do "back in the old days."

Unfortunately, that sink-or-swim strategy is one of the biggest reasons companies have employees who have no idea what they are doing or how they should act with customers. I'd bet that the next time you have a bad customer experience, there is a 50% chance the employee is new to their role in the past 30 days. A poor orientation and onboarding is also why we lose some of our best new talent so quickly and have such high turnover costs. According to business and productivity expert Stephanie Vozza, more than 40% of turnover happens within the first month, and another 10% or more of new hires leave before their first year. There are real costs associated with this quick turnover, with Vozza putting that cost at three times an annual salary when you consider the costs of recruiting, hiring, and training someone else.[2]

Let's talk about what your orientation and onboarding program and process should look like. First, be sure to differentiate the two. I define orientation as someone's first one or two days on the job and onboarding as the process of getting staff members trained and socialized into a new role and the overall culture, a process generally occurring over 30–60 days. Please note that some specialist roles may require a longer initial training process, but within those first 60 days, both new employees and the organization should know whether a long-term relationship is possible.

We believe that the first day of an associate's new job should be a great experience and the next 60 days should be about teaching him or her to deliver great experiences to your customers.

A Memorable Orientation Experience

The orientation should be memorable, motivating, and effective in introducing new employees to the brand, culture, and business. Horst Schulze, the former CEO of The Ritz-Carlton Hotel Company, instilled into the company's managers that a person's first day on a job is one of those times when they will be most open to change and to do what managers tell them to do. The first day on the job is when new hires consciously or subconsciously learn the priorities of the company. What experience do your new staff members receive on their first day, and what priorities are you communicating?

When you place your new staff members on the front line immediately, you are communicating to them that the only thing that matters is getting a job done, regardless of quality or customer satisfaction. The focus is on the transaction, completed in an average way at best, rather than any sort of customer experience.

For companies that do have some sort of first-day orientation experience, often that first day is uninspiring (new hires spend it reading all those rules and signing paperwork), disorganized (no one realized they were starting that day), or a waste of time (they sit on the sidelines while team members are too busy to care that they arrived). As a result, many people's first impressions of a new company are poor, to say the least. But no one ever blames the lack of an orientation for team members quitting quickly—they blame the modern workers' lack of work ethic and loyalty. In reality, new hires who leave quickly are the smart ones who get out before wasting too much of their time.

How can this bland first impression be improved? Companies can start by taking care of the paperwork online prior to someone's first day; this includes sending out employment information, tax forms, benefits packages, and other miscellaneous paperwork. Don't let the first day be focused on completing required paperwork that, with a little more preparation, could have been finalized beforehand. Remember that if all new people do on their first day is paperwork, they will quickly understand that paperwork is most important to the company.

Managing new-hire paperwork and ongoing employee files is another area where technology is making a difference. A number of human resources software programs are available that can start to manage and organize employees' paperwork before they begin work, eliminating the necessity of using an employee's first day to complete paperwork and collect information. Some examples include BambooHR, ClearCompany, and Zenefits. As Ramon Garcia, an account manager for Zenefits, recently told us, "Today, employers are realizing that an energetic and effective start to a new job is a key factor in attracting and retaining top talent, boosting productivity, and driving business growth."[3] The bottom line is, we need to be spending less time on compliance and paperwork and more time on setting up staff members with a great first impression of the organization.

Speaking of first impressions, I also suggest spending less time focusing on the rules in day 1. By inundating new hires with rules, the message is clear—following the rules is the most important thing to us, no matter what. One exception to the rule about rules is if the brand is Nordstrom or a company with a similar perspective on rules. Nordstrom has just one rule, and that is: "Use your best judgment in all situations. There will be no additional rules."[4] This rule puts customers first, but for many service-oriented companies, an early focus on rules often means that although employees will be good with rules, they will not be so good with customers or connecting to your brand.

So, what should day 1 look like? I have been involved with many organizations in developing the best possible first-day experience for employees. As a result of my experience, I suggest that you focus on four things during your new employees' first day.

1. Introduce Your Brand

On day 1, introduce the company's products, services, and, most important, its customers. I often refer to the company's mission as the first and most important message new hires get on their first day. Your mission statement should clearly state what your company does and for whom. I want to make this clear—if you can't articulate this simply and easily, then you have a problem. Knowing what your company does and who its customers are is the most fundamental and important piece of information a person receives on their first day. In addition, the same information should be constantly reinforced with your current team. Never let your people forget what they do and for whom they are doing it.

When I ask companies what they do and for whom they are working, I am either given a mission statement that is too marketing driven and therefore not easily understood, or there is no answer at all. A mission statement may be the simplest and most basic statement about your organization, but for your new employees, it may also be the most important. It also may bring clarity to your whole organization. We worked with a large real estate company that did not have a mission statement. Working with the owners, we developed a statement as part of the new-hire orientation program. However, as it was communicated throughout the organization, executives and managers expressed their appreciation for finally putting the stake in the ground about what the focus of the company really was.

The next step is to focus in on what makes the company or the products and services it offers unique. I refer to these as the company pillars—those things that make you stand out in your customers' eyes. I often bundle these two elements, the mission and pillars, into the company's customer promise. You are promising to provide something to someone in a specific way to make them satisfied, delighted, or raving fans.

If we are going to begin with the brand and focus on the customer, ensure that sales and marketing people are involved in this presentation. Let new staff members see or experience a sales presentation about the products and services they will be responsible for. Help them understand the importance of their role in fulfilling the company and customer promise. However, as I have noted, a word of caution: Sometimes the marketing version of a mission, position statement, pillars, or vision can be creatively driven and offer little clarity to staff about what the company does and what sets it apart. In these situations, I often help the marketing team create a simplified and more straightforward version that new hires can easily digest.

2. Define and Showcase Your Customer Experience and Expectations

It is important to introduce new hires to the desired customer experience. In an ideal world, new team members would be able to observe customer interactions, hear customer feedback, and see other staff members in action. You want your new hires to understand what the preferred outcome is—a happy customer—and how they impact that outcome. Take them on a tour and let them observe. As we highly recommend not spending the whole first day in a classroom, this is a great excuse to go for a walk and to emphasize the importance of the customer. Another best practice we have seen utilized by some organizations is to show a video that involves real life customers talking about what is important and how staff can make a difference in keeping them happy. Let your new people know what your customers expect and what the company has promised to deliver.

3. Give a History Lesson

Culture is reinforced through storytelling and an understanding of the company's history. Take some time to talk about what makes people working in your company most proud. It is also important to recount the company's history and a few key moments that have defined your success. This is a great opportunity to have other staff members come in and provide their own stories or an overview of the company's history, especially if they have been around awhile. If possible, involve the owners or a senior executive as well. Ari Weinzweig, CEO of Zingerman's Delicatessen said: "By taking the time to teach the orientation, the clear message that comes across is that we value [new employees] and their work so highly that the head of the company is willing to sit with them to go over things."[5] Involving owners or executive officers in orientations is a powerful first impression for new staff.

4. Introduce Values

And finally, it is important to introduce company values to new staff on their first day. Doing this ensures they understand that *how* things are done is just as important as *what* is done. This introduction should not consist of just handing out a sheet of paper or card with the values printed on it. Instead, bring the values to life in a fun, imaginative, and meaningful way. Over the years, we have utilized videos, fables, games, discussions, and role-plays to introduce values. We always recap each exercise with a discussion and some reflection on what each value means to team members. As an organization, we probably have had our most fun in coming up with different and diverse activities to bring a company's values to life. Using our example values from Chapter 2, Table 4.1 shows some examples of what we might do to introduce them.

We recommend that you bring in a variety of current staff or managers to help facilitate the games or discussions about what each value means. Doing this not only highlights to the listeners the importance of the values but it helps those delivering the messages to understand their values better. Education and discussion of values should take up the majority of the time on the first day and be the most memorable lesson.

Commit to making day 1 something new employees talk about, tweet about, or even rave about. Robert Mellwig, senior vice president of Really Cool People for Two Roads Hospitality, a hotel management company, said, "We work hard at the first day experience. We strive to create a welcoming environment and a full cultural immersion."[9] Focus on making new team members the company's biggest fans; after all, isn't that what you hope team members will do for customers in the future?

If the first day, orientation, is about delivering a great experience to your new staff, then the next 60 days are about teaching them to deliver a great experience to either their internal or external customers.

An Effective Onboarding Process

Once the first day(s) is (are) out of the way, new employees move into their departments to begin their official onboarding process. Unfortunately, however, things tend go wrong here as well. Even when there is a great orientation day in place, managed and organized by the HR team, once new employees are handed over to their departments, it often seems as if they walked into the unknown and unprepared. Consider onboarding a certification process, in that after this period of time, you are certain that new employees can complete the job or tasks required in such a way as to be aligned with the company values.

Table 4.1 Sample Activities to Bring Your Values to Life

Creative: Nothing Is Impossible	Collaborative: Contribute and Support
Video: *Apollo 13*[6] Show clips from the film *Apollo 13* that highlight the task of bringing the astronauts back to Earth, how the scientists went about the seemingly impossible task, and the creativity employed to achieve the impossible. The final scenes when Apollo 13 makes it back to Earth are also motivating. The main message is that in this real-life situation, under the most difficult of circumstances, when people come together and think creatively, nothing is impossible.	**Game:** "Win as Much as You Can"[7] This game challenges participants on their competitiveness, collaboration, communication, and, most important, who they think their team is. This activity stresses that regardless of an employee's department, all employees are part of a larger company team and must look to win as a company, not as a department to the detriment of another department.
Accountable: Ask for Forgiveness, Not Permission	**Passionate: Love What You Do or Why Bother?**
Activity: "Wilderness Survival"[8] This game teaches participants how to make good decisions as a team by stressing the importance of time, leadership, expertise, objectives, and outcomes. The main message is that when making decisions, people should utilize all the resources, talents, time, and common sense they have to come up with the best possible decision. The decision may not be perfect, but as long as people use a common methodology, they will make the best possible decision in that moment.	**Activity:** "Share Your Passions" Have participants sit with someone they do not know well and share their passions for one minute each. It is amazing how quickly people become connected or feel they know each other when they know what or who they love. Also, most of the time, participants find passions in common. People start to become real when you know what their passions are. It is important to do this with your peers and customers to build the type of relationships that will truly make a difference.

Ron Thomas, an HR strategy consultant, says:

> When we're talking about onboarding and an employee's first
> ninety days on the job, what we're really talking about is
> employee retention. . . . Without a proper plan for bringing
> new employees on board, managers run the risk of mis-
> communication of goals and expectations, sub-par performance,
> lower morale, bad decisions and potentially financial loss in the
> form of employee turnover.[10]

Now, most of the time when you hear about onboarding, it is
referring to the first 90 days; however, as I mentioned earlier, I focus on
60 days, because that is about the time when new associates determine
whether they are going to stay with the company long term. Consider
that, according to *HR Morning* editor Christian Schappel, 31% of
people quit in the first six months, and more than half of those quit in
the first 60 days.[11] Also remember that this is the time companies
should be deciding if they want an employee to stay as well. Not every
hire you make is the right one, so, while new staffers are still making up
their minds about your company, you should ensure the onboarding
process allows you to do the same of them.

Let's consider what a good onboarding program looks like. Once an
employee is handed over to his or her respective department or team,
the first thing to consider is how prepared and welcoming the department or team is of the new hire. How the rest of the team welcomes the
new person into the department tells them how important they are and
will play a big part in their mindset over the first few days. How many
times does a new person turn up in a department and the team was
unaware anyone was even hired? How often is there no desk ready to be
used, computer ready to go, or welcoming note to be seen? Make new
associates feel welcome—have their work area or space organized with
the tools ready to do the job, and add a note or gift and proper
introductions.

The next thing to consider is who is responsible for orienting the
new associate to the department and answering questions. One best
practice for the first day or week in the department is to assign a mentor
to the new hire. An appropriate mentor would be a person with a

similar job function or someone with similar skills and competencies who can act as a resource for the new employee. Mentoring also fosters new relationships and strengthens ties within your organization. The University of Virginia found that connecting new employees with mentors encourages job commitment. Including a mentorship program in the onboarding of new employees is important for connecting them to the team, processes, and culture.[12]

The next thing to consider within your onboarding program is how new associates are introduced and connected with the products or services they now represent, deliver, or sell. It is important to ensure that new staff members have a chance to try out the products and services themselves. Doing this allows new team members to know that their confidence and comfort with products and services is important, and it sets the expectation that regardless of their position, they are ambassadors, users, and salespeople. When I worked in hotels, management would often ensure new employees had the chance to stay a night to experience what guests experience. At some automotive dealerships where we have worked, team members are given a chance to take cars home during their first week for a thorough test drive. Retail stores often provide their staff with clothes from the latest line to understand the style and quality intimately. How is your brand connecting new staff members to what they ultimately are servicing or selling?

The majority of the first 60 days is spent training new staffers to get them familiar with the tasks and responsibilities of their new roles, especially with customers. We cover training in more detail in Chapter 5, but for new hires, there are five important questions to answer.

1. Who Is Going to Train?

As a manager, get comfortable training new people and contributing to their growth and development. However, due to other responsibilities, managers cannot be expected to have regular training roles. I find that training programs, especially for new hires, are most effective when someone other than the manager trains team members as it allows for uninterrupted and focused training. Identify a person who exemplifies the skills and behaviors to be developed—someone who displays a positive disposition about the service experience and about helping others. At The Ritz-Carlton Hotel Company, each department had a trainer, an employee who exemplified what to do and how to do it. This trainer was paired up with new hires on the second day and stayed with them until they completed their onboarding process. This method allowed managers to be coaches—which we talk about in Chapter 6—with someone else, generally a potential manager, taking on the training role. This was a win-win-win for the new hire, trainer, and manager and a best practice we highly encourage in other companies.

2. Where Will Training Be Provided?

Training must be conducted in an environment that minimizes distractions and interruptions. Particularly when new information is being taught, it is important to begin training away from the real-world work environment. The fault of many new-hire training programs is that they place trainees on the front lines immediately to learn as they go. This is not effective or practical until after trainees have developed some form of understanding and comprehension of the job and tasks as well as confidence in their surroundings. Ensure the training area is conducive to learning, with the temperature appropriate and seating available. Be organized. Have any necessary training tools ready for trainees' use.

This is a good opportunity to talk about training rooms, or, as I often refer to them, those places where learning goes to die. The training rooms, those often forgotten back rooms used for day-1 orientations are generally non-branded, uninspiring, and not conducive to learning. If we are going to introduce the brand and culture and get our new people excited about where they are working and the brand they are working for then maybe it would be a good idea to add a little style, creativity, and branding to your training rooms. They should reflect your brand so build in a sensory experience that is reflective of your customers. What your new people see, smell, hear, touch, and taste on their first day sets the foundation of their expectations so make the room in which orientation occurs something special. Add posters, color, and motivational thoughts to the walls. Ensure the desks and chairs are comfortable. Additional ideas could be to play music, apply aromatherapy, and offer an upgraded dining experience on day 1 to help make it memorable. Consider an investment in your training environment to make it more than an afterthought and something not important.

3. When Will Training Happen?

With new hires, there must be a clearly defined training period in which all the necessary information and skills are to be covered. Each day should include new processes, a review of previous material, and an introduction to people in the department and to those in other departments with whom they will work closely. Provide new staff with a schedule for training that clearly indicates start and finish times and what will be learned each day.

4. What Is Going to Be Taught?

As we have suggested, start with how to interact with customers. Obviously, managers need to begin a thorough training of all the processes and rules of the job as well. Standardize all the tasks and processes the team is responsible for and ensure they are updated regularly. Dale Turner, a hospitality advisor, wrote: "If you don't define (and train) precisely what is supposed to happen when a customer encounters an organization at any given point, then the experience will at best be mediocre."[13] Remember also that each discussion of customer interactions, processes, and rules of the job provides another opportunity to clearly demonstrate how the values and associated behaviors should be implemented on a daily basis.

When building a training program for your new hires, don't forget to provide some cross-training with other departments they will be working closely with. New hires may have to spend as little as an hour for an overview of what a particular department or role does, but it will supply firsthand understanding of how everyone needs to work together.

Having a clearly defined learning map for each position is probably one of the most important onboarding resources a manager and the organization can have. Knowing exactly what needs to be trained and how long it takes is critical to ensuring your new hires are set up for success. Once we were asked to work with a small hotel company to look at why there were so many inconsistencies in service standards and customer experiences across the brand, as indicated by surveys and mystery shop reports. When we reviewed all the cultural mechanisms, we found that the issues with service were mainly a result of the inconsistencies within the onboarding process. New staff members were being taught about the brand's service standards differently and at different stages of the onboarding process. By developing a single learning map by position of what was to be trained at all properties, the brand feedback from customers became more consistent and the experience was more positive.

Be sure that you have a detailed outline of the schedule of who, where, when, and what for onboarding new employees. For a great example of an effective schedule, see our Culture Hacker Onboarding Plan in Figure 4.1.

Activity	Position A	Position B	Position C	Position D
Week 1				
Orientation: Welcome, tour, meet with leadership team, meet with mentor	Day 1	Day 1	Day 1	Day 1
Cultural Immersion	Day 2	Day 2	Day 2	Day 2
Service Training	Day 3	Day 3	Day 3	Day 3
Leadership Training	Day 4	Day 4	Day 4	X
Advanced Service Training	X	X	X	Day 4
Technology Training	Day 5	Day 5	Day 5	Day 5
Weeks 2–3				
Shadowing rotation through key departments				
Week 4				
Department shadowing/training Informal 30-day review				
Weeks 5–7				
Department shadowing/training				Start working on own in position
Week 8				
Working on own in position Formal Review				

Figure 4.1   Onboarding Plan

Consider at the end of each new employees' onboarding program some sort of testing. Ensure that what you expected to be taught has in fact been taught. I have seen more and more organizations add in testing components to the onboarding process to ensure that the new staff members are meeting expectations regarding an ability to learn. I found that by letting new staff know they are going to be tested throughout the first 60 days that they are more likely to pay attention and apply themselves in the beginning. Any test does not need to be difficult but should be challenging enough to have credibility. The certification process for each employee must be audited to ensure that each department and manager is setting up their new people for success.

5. How Will We Get Feedback?

The final element of the onboarding program is to ensure you get feedback from new hires that what you promised in their onboarding experience did in fact happen. Begin with informal opportunities to get a pulse on how new associates are doing and feeling. By the 60-day mark, managers should have a pretty good feel for what the new employees' experiences have been like and the direction they're heading with the company. However, it is a good idea to formalize the feedback from a new hire with a 60-day employee review to set strategic goals for the new employee's next 6 to 12 months.

The 60-day employee review should include a portion for new employees to complete regarding their new employee experience. Doing so creates an opportunity for new team members to reflect on how *their* values align with those of the organization and their fit with the organization. The 60-day mark is the right time for both the new employee and the manager to assess the long-term relationship and opportunities between the employee and the company.

One best practice I have been a big supporter of is the graduation ceremony. At the end of onboarding, once a new employee has been certified in their position, make a big deal about it. This not only makes your new employee feel good but it also signifies to them that more is and can be expected of them. One organization provides new staff with their official uniform upon graduating, which shows they are now ready to make a difference. By offering a uniform upgrade, change to their name tag, a certificate, or even just some recognition from the team, signifying the end of onboarding with some fun and ceremony is worth the time and effort.

Remember that even if new staff members are happy in their first 60 days that they are still prone to leave during their first year, so don't stop checking in with your new people on their employee experience. Make the onboarding process ongoing during the whole first year. As Ben Peterson, CEO of Bamboo HR, said, "Orientation is not a single event. It's an ongoing talent strategy."[14] Not only does a great orientation and onboarding program set your new people up for success, but it also significantly enhances your employer brand and reputation. One company whose reputation has been enhanced by the way it onboards staff and introduces its values is Netflix, the focus of the following case study.

Case Study: Netflix

With over 75 million subscribers streaming content in more than 190 countries, Netflix has become a popular culture phenomenon.[15] When the company launched in April 1998, it only had 30 employees; as of 2015, Netflix employs over 3,500 employees and is worth over $2 billion. Part of this multinational entertainment company's success is tied to how it immerses new employees in their values and culture and sets up new people for success. However, a big part of Netflix's success with new staff is how this process begins even before a person's first day.

Netflix is well-known for their culture deck introducing their company values and behaviors. They wanted to ensure that those thinking about or having joined the company understand how important their values are. Freedom and responsibility are key tenets of the culture, which, Netflix readily admits, is not for everyone.[16] By focusing on their key tenets, potential or new hires self-select themselves.

Netflix conducts prework to ensure each employee is set up for success on his or her first day. Employees are contacted prior to starting to provide their computer preference and any particular software needs.[17] Employees arrive on their first day to find everything set up and ready to go. This gesture not only makes the employees feel welcome, but it also sets the tone that support is provided so that employees can focus on performing and delivering results. Managers are held responsible for having a great team, thus they take an active approach to onboarding their new employees effectively.

Employees are introduced to key people from their own and other departments. New employees are assigned a mentor. Within the first month of

(continued)

(*continued*)

working for Netflix, new hires meet with senior executives in small informal group settings to get to know each other and re-emphasize the company's aspirations.[17]

Netflix's high performance culture is not for everyone, but the company ensures that when they select great people, they invest the time and resources to make new hires successful, something a lot of other companies could learn to do better.

Now is the time to do a quick review of your onboarding program—do you deliver? Don't assume every department has an organized and thorough process for getting new talent up to speed. Consider what is happening throughout your organization.

The goal is to have a great first day for your new employees, one they remember and talk about and that establishes the priorities for your company or team. Then you must build on the orientation by having a thorough and organized onboarding schedule that gives all new staff members a chance to contribute the right way. I believe that the orientation and onboarding process is about making a great first impression for your new employees. They have made the decision to come and work and are ready to be impressed and molded. Now it's up to you to deliver.

Let's commit as leaders to stop utilizing the outdated sink-or-swim strategy that wastes our resources and the great talent we worked so hard to hire. Take the time to invest in your orientation and onboarding programs and set your people up for success. Exceed your new employees' expectations so that they can, in turn, do the same for your customers and for you.

Culture Hack: Introduce and immerse your new employees so they are emotionally connected to the company and are set up for success.

1. Make your orientation or day 1 an experience for new employees that introduces them to the products, services, customer brand, and culture.
2. Develop an onboarding plan that includes training, mentorship, and both informal and formal performance reviews in the first 60 days.
3. Clarify for each position exactly what a new employee needs to master in order to complete the job and demonstrate the company values. Develop tests throughout the onboarding process to ensure learning is occurring.
4. Include in your onboarding plan the details on who is training, where training will occur, when training will occur, and what is being trained.
5. Capture your new employees' feedback at 30 and 60 days to ensure that you are meeting their expectations and delivering on your employee promise.

Notes

1. J. K. Rowling, *Harry Potter and the Order of the Phoenix* (New York: Scholastic, 2003).
2. Stephanie Vozza, "What to Do During Your Employees' First Week to Avoid Losing Them," *FastCompany*, May 9, 2016. https://www.fastcompany.com/3059585/what-to-do-during-your-employees-first-week-to-avoid-losing-them
3. Ramon Garcia, email message to author, December 12, 2016.
4. Micah Solomon, "Take These Two Steps to Rival Nordstrom's Customer Service Experience," *Forbes*, March 15, 2014. http://www.forbes.com/sites/micahsolomon/2014/03/15/the-nordstrom-two-part-customer-experience-formula-lessons-for-your-business
5. Quoted in Peter Vanden Bos, "How to Build an Onboarding Plan for a New Hire," *Inc.* (April 2010). http://www.inc.com/guides/2010/04/building-an-onboarding-plan.html
6. *Apollo 13*. Film. Directed by Ron Howard. 1995. Universal City, CA: Universal Pictures, 2005. DVD.

7. W. Gellermann, "Win as Much as You Can: An Intergroup Competition," Part 2, Section 3 of *Pfeiffer's Classic Activities: Managing Conflict at Work* (Hoboken, NJ: John Wiley & Sons, 2003).

8. "SURVIVAL: A Simulation Game." ScoutingWeb.com, n.d. http://scoutingweb.com/scoutingweb/SubPages/SurvivalGame.htm

9. *Culture Hacker* podcast, 2017. Season 1, Episode 1. On-air talent includes: Robert Mellwig, Shane Green.

10. Quoted in Lou Dubois, "How to Make an Employee's First 90 Days Successful." *Inc.* (December 2010). http://www.inc.com/guides/2010/12/how-to-make-an-employees-first-90-days-successful.html

11. Christian Schappel, "5 Biggest Reasons Employees Quit Jobs Quickly," *HRMorning*, May 20, 2016. http://www.hrmorning.com/5-biggest-reasons-employees-quit-jobs-quickly

12. University of Virginia Career Center, "Mentoring." https://career.virginia.edu/networking/mentoring

13. Dale M. Turner, "On the Matter of Leadership," *Hotel Online* (April 2002). http://www.hotel-online.com/Trends/TurnKey/MatterOfLeadership.html

14. Roy Maurer, "Onboarding Key to Retaining, Engaging Talent," *SHRM* (April 2015). https://www.shrm.org/resourcesandtools/hr-topics/talent-acquisition/pages/onboarding-key-retaining-engaging-talent.aspx

15. Ben Popper, "Netflix Whizzes Past 75 Million Subscribers Thanks to Record International Growth" January 1, 2016. http://www.theverge.com/2016/1/19/10790282/netflix-q4-2015-earnings

16. Patty McCord, "How Netflix Reinvents HR" (January 2014). https://hbr.org/2014/01/how-netflix-reinvented-hr

17. Justin Reynolds, "3 Companies with the Most Unique Employee Onboarding Practices" (March 2016). https://www.tinypulse.com/blog/companies-with-the-most-unique-employee-onboarding-practices

5

Performance Management

How We Fail to Maximize Our Employees' Abilities and Talents

To command is to serve, nothing more and nothing less.
—Andre Malraux, French novelist[1]

FOR THE SUCCESS OF YOUR business you must enable and empower your people to maximize their abilities and strengths, and to maximize their performance.

When it comes to an employee's performance in a professional context we often hear the term "performance management" being used. I believe just by using the word "management" within this term it causes many employees to underperform and many managers to underdeliver in their responsibility to get the best out of their people. The *Merriam-Webster* dictionary defines "management" as "the act or skill of controlling and making decisions about a business, department, sports team, etc."[2] I suggest the "etc." includes people. So, if we are going to control and make decisions around performance, I think we are causing our staff and the business to underperform. Underperformance and wasting talents are real issues—if you are not convinced, ask your customers, both internal and external. So many companies and managers try to control their people and make decisions for them; it is no wonder their staffers turn off and adopt a passive or indifferent attitude.

We have to rethink performance in the workplace. Instead of trying to control our people and make decisions for them—which, let's face it, creates a very narrow and mundane mindset—we need to do exactly the opposite, we need to unleash it. We propose to replace the word "management" with two words that are more in line with what we should be trying to achieve: performance enablement and performance empowerment. HR expert Michelle Crosby said it best on our *Culture Hacker* podcast: "Give people the space, the tools, the latitude they need to get their job done. Give people the power to act in a way that they know their job needs to be done."[3] As managers, we must enable our people to do their jobs and unleash their talents by providing them with what they need to be successful. We then need to empower them by getting out of the way and allowing them to be in control and responsible for delivering the desired results in the right way.

In this chapter, I consider how to define performance and then how to enable and to empower your people to maximize their and the company's performance. Let's begin by defining performance. Managers talk extensively about performance, yet when I ask them to describe what performance really is or what they want their employees to achieve, confusion quickly sets in and a diverse set of answers are provided. How can we get your people perform when you can't even accurately describe what we want them to do and how they should do it? This is the first problem—you must define what performance is before you can begin to elevate performance across your company or team. So, let's clarify what performance should look like.

Defining Performance

Company objectives should be directly aligned with the performance managers wish to see from the staff. Depending on each employee's role, these objectives should be contributing directly to the financial bottom line, market share, customer satisfaction, employee satisfaction, or the company's position in the community. We talk more about this in Chapter 7 when discussing company strategy, scores, and plans. For now, just know that the objectives or the goals of each employee must be aligned with the overall objectives and goals of the organization.

Once the goals have been set by a company, managers must establish relevant goals for each employee based on his or her ability to impact each of the main objectives. Depending on their job roles, employees may have different perspectives on what good performance is for them. If team members have no influence on the company's financial position—that is, if they are unable to generate new or repeat sales or minimize expenses—then don't judge their perform- ance on the company's financial position. However, say the employ- ees have an opportunity to impact both sales via upselling and customer satisfaction through their interaction. Managers might determine that performance for them is 35% based on achieving an upsell or cross-sell goal and 65% on customer feedback and satisfaction. For many roles, these scores may be a part of a group or departmental overall score rather than something that can be individually tracked, although it is becoming more common for companies to evaluate individual performance metrics as well.

Once the desired results from each position or team are established, you have half of the performance equation (in other words, *how much* they have to deliver). Next, consider *how* team members deliver it. We have all met people who absolutely nail their metric goals while simultaneously destroying the morale and success of everyone else around them. Now we need to think about the other important performance element—company values.

If you recall from Chapter 2, values define how team members act and interact with their organization, customers, and peers. Defining how all employees in the company should act and interact is non- negotiable in today's world. Unfortunately in the past couple of years, we heard about and saw situations like the Wells Fargo fake account scandal,[4] whereby these companies placed too much emphasis on the "how much" over the "how to." In today's transparent business environ- ment, we have to ensure that we prioritize how we act and interact as defined by our values just as much as we prioritize our need to get things done and achieve results. We need balance, which should be reflected in how performance is defined.

By utilizing company values, managers can define how team members should achieve their goals and thus defining the other half of the performance equation. The job of a manager is to help team members achieve the desired level of performance. As team members reach their goals in the right way, managers should continue to stretch and challenge them to achieve higher levels of performance by setting higher goals without sacrificing company values and integrity.

Performance Enablement

According to the Merriam-Webster dictionary, "enable" is about making someone (or something) able to do or to be something.[5] I love the idea of organizations enabling their staff to achieve their desired performance goals. To enable your people, you need to provide them with the training, tools, information, and feedback necessary to perform. The role of managers is to serve their people, not the other way around. Serving their people means enabling them to be successful. Nothing helps to get the desired results faster than managers who are clear about what they want to achieve, passionate about the results, and committed to doing whatever it takes to allow their team to perform their respective roles at the highest levels. According to Herb Kelleher, the former chairman of Southwest Airlines, "Leadership is being a faithful, devoted, and hardworking servant of the people you lead."[6]

Let's consider the ways we can serve our people best in more detail.

Training

The first aspect of enabling your team is to ensure they have the right training. For the past 16 years, I have been creating classroom and online training modules that develop skills, growth, and a passion for learning. Over that time, I have learned a lot about what makes a great learning experience.

In Chapter 4, we discussed the importance of onboarding people and providing initial training for them to do the job. What managers cannot do is think that once the onboarding or certification is complete, their training responsibilities are over. Staff members require constant training and exposure to learning to remain relevant, open minded, and up-to-date with their customers, new technology, and the state of the business. Research, experience, financial results, and customer satisfaction scores speak to the value of continuously training team members.

When it comes to training, an important area of focus should be on the values and behaviors that you have identified as the foundation of your business. In Chapter 2, we defined four values. One was "creative." For this value to have meaning within your organization, you should invest in training that allows your people to be creative, open to new ideas, and solution focused (knowing how to ask good questions). In other words, training must support the behaviors associated with the foundational values. This type of training and learning can come from articles, books, speakers, or others within your company. Another value was "passionate," which can include training around how to have a positive mindset, manage stress, or kick-start a career.

Regardless of your organizational values, a focus on providing training that enhances people's lives in general helps to create the right company culture. We worked with an organization in the Caribbean, and one focus of training was to teach employees financial responsibility and familiarity to support the company's goal of enhancing the lives of those in their local community. This investment in time and resources did little to enhance employees' skills on the job but was incredible in terms of ensuring that staff members felt connected and engaged with the business and what it was trying to do, which was deliver great customer service.

Another example of a company where an investment in training can impact not only what happens at work but also how people run their lives is Starbucks. Starbucks has invested heavily in life skills and coping mechanisms for its staff. In his book *The Power of Habit*, Charles Duhigg describes the process of training Starbucks staff on the habit of self-discipline, which not only supported the organization's growth strategy but improved customer satisfaction and, most important, cultivated a highly empowered and engaged workforce. The training employees received not only impacted them professionally but personally as well. Duhigg concluded: "Starbucks—like a handful of other companies—has succeeded in teaching the kind of life skills that schools, families, and communities have failed to provide."[7]

Regardless of the disgruntled few staffers committed to remaining in the status quo, most team members, especially young ones, crave training and, in many instances, quit because of a lack of development. eLearningindustry.com reported that 25% of employees leave their jobs because there aren't enough training or development opportunities.[8] To get people to perform, give them what they want—an opportunity to learn and grow.

Now, it is important to avoid thinking of training as some sort of magic bean that will instantly transform your people into something special or even make them capable. Learning requires time—30 days to break habits, 30 days to adopt new habits, and continuous reinforcement through feedback. I adhere to a 60/20/20 model for learning that defines the requirements for learning as 60% done on the job, 20% from feedback and coaching, and 20% from formal training.

The 60%, or on-the-job learning, is by far the most impactful learning opportunity because it is based on experience. American educator Edgar Dale developed the Cone of Experience concept, which explains that two weeks after a learning event, learners will most likely remember 10% of what they read (passive learning), 20% of what they heard (passive learning), 30% of what they saw (passive learning), 50% of what they saw and heard (passive learning), 70% of what they said (active learning), and 90% of what they did (experiential learning).[9]

There is no better way for your people to learn than by getting on the front line and actually doing—but this is where your investments in a good onboarding program, in mentoring or dedicated trainers, and in opportunities to gain experience in a safe environment away from customers are so important. One restaurant we worked with set up training tables where the owners or managers ate. New staff members were given these tables to practice on in a relatively safe environment (although they still were pressured to deliver exceptional service). Another client of ours manages call centers, and the company set up a phone system for new trainees that is connected to internal phones only. Managers were given various scenarios and a schedule to call in. Calls were recorded and then reviewed by the employee and the trainer, who provided great insights into how the employee was doing. Again, these realistic interactions did not impact real customers, so new employees could practice in a safe environment.

We review coaching (20%) in Chapter 6, so I will resist talking about this for now. Let's consider what formal training (20%) should look like to emphasize learning. In our experience, it is important to provide a hands-on learning experience during classroom or online training. This means the training provides participants with the opportunity to consider concepts and business cases; engage in role-plays, group discussions, and games; and reflect on and define how they would put the lessons into practice. In alignment with Malcolm Knowles's adult learning theory, I believe that all participants in training are self-directed learners who are oriented for personal and professional goals, value mutual respect, and bring life skills and experience to the shared learning experience.[10]

Another consideration for formal training sessions is to limit time in a classroom. Training should no longer be eight hours a day sitting in one room listening to a single voice lecture or read from a single perspective. Learning must be delivered in short, inspirational, effective, and fun sessions that last no more than 90 to 120 minutes per interval. Training needs to involve multiple mediums or voices integrated into video, games, discussions, and role-plays that develop understanding of and familiarity with the desired ideas or habits. A large retail client provides a mixture of online formal training and on-the-floor live training during its various modules. This method ensures there is a balance of formal training, on-the-job experience, and coaching whenever something new is introduced to their stores.

Traditionally, a lot of formal training has occurred in the classroom. Today, however, it is necessary to ensure you are also making online training or e-learning readily available. A lot of managers, when they initially hear the word "e-learning," are not impressed, due to some of their early experiences with online modules that were bland, not on brand, and lacked any interactivity. Things have certainly changed, with on-line learning now able to play an integral part in an employee's learning and development due to advances in design and software ability.

The Sales Readiness Group found that most learners will forget 80% of the training material within 90 to 120 days after delivery of the training unless there is a strong reinforcement program in place.[11] E-learning is excellent for reinforcing training that occurs in the classroom or actual operation. It is a quick way of reviewing key learning ideas, skills, or desired habits. As an important note for all companies interested in developing their service cultures, the research group Bersin & Associates found in 2012 that e-learning results in 34% better response to customer needs and 26% greater ability to deliver "quality products" and services.[12]

The real advantage of online training is that it can be completed on tablets and phones, where staff members can access it most easily. We have developed modules for tablets that have shown housekeepers how to clean rooms and bartenders how to set up a bar. These tablet-based learning experiences mean that training is happening with the act of delivery. Continuing with this idea, some of the best training is available on smartphones, where employees can interact with the software and get feedback on how they are doing. We have been developing content for such a software platform for some time. Star Coach by Forbes Travel is an app that analyzes voice recordings for various scenarios. According to Peter Kressaty, senior vice president for Forbes Travel, "It helps users be aware of their emotional state and adjust their mindset to be most effective and genuine in guest interactions."[13] This type of simulator-based training is the way forward for training in the future.

For formal training, a combination of classroom, software, and online learning opportunities works best. If you are serious about enabling your staff, you must be committed to investing in the skills and development of your people. Nespresso, the leading European single-serve coffee brand, is a great example of how providing training and development helps enable and empower employees.

Case Study: Nespresso

Although part of the larger parent company Nestlé, Nespresso, a European single-serve gourmet coffee brand, established its own culture, one of diversity, innovation, and growth.[14] The company realized that the development of their people also develops the brand. Through enabling and empowering their staff, the Nespresso employees are committed to not only building their careers, but also to building the brand. Nespresso is now present in 64 countries and has more than 12,000 employees worldwide, up from only 331 in 2000.

Enablement at Nespresso is a result of the training provided to all employees. To start, employees are trained on all necessary "core factors" needed to be successful in their role. These core functions include product and company knowledge, job knowledge, and leadership skills.

Nespresso's extensive product-knowledge training program extends to all of its more than 7,000 employees. Each employee is trained on the "science of coffee," learning how Nespresso is produced every step of the way. The training involves a tasting of the 16 core flavors sold by the company. The purpose of the course is to "offer employees a chance to understand and appreciate Nespresso's expertise in the selection, roasting, and blending processes," according to Renaud Tinel, Nespresso Oceania General Manager and Market Director.[15] An important outcome of this product training is the connection employees feel to the organization. As Tinel explains, "Training helps employees understand where they fit in the big picture and how exactly they contribute to the overall business objectives." This result is in line with research that demonstrates that training results in happy, informed, and engaged employees.[16]

The training at Nespresso does not stop at product knowledge. "Our priority is to integrate our employees and provide them with all the training necessary for their current job as well as ensuring their future development," said Stephanie Coduys, Learning and Development Manager.[17] Employees are encouraged to grow with the company and are provided support in the form of new opportunities for experiential learning, mentorship, and formal training.

Next, employees develop their "accelerators," which help fuel their career and prepare them for opportunities. Accelerators include gaining cross-functional skills and networking needed to take advantage of opportunities.[18] The company follows the 70/20/10 model when designing their high-quality development plans. Like what was described earlier in this chapter, 70% is based on experience-based activity, 20% is based on coaching and feedback, and 10% is based on formal training. Nespresso has found that this model helps to fully and quickly develop individuals in their career.[18] Nespresso empowers their employees by providing a wide sphere of influence and allowing them the freedom to make decisions.[18]

The investment in job, company, leadership, and cross-functional skills ensures Nespresso staff are set up for success in their current role as well as in additional roles in the future. The focus on training to enable staff and help them make good decisions should be a foundation of every organization.

The Tools to Do the Job

If you are serious about enabling your people, then you have to ensure they have the tools to do the job. How many times have your employees frustrated a customer and failed in delivering a great experience because they didn't have the right or enough tools and resources to do their jobs? Such failures are also are good ways to frustrate employees and ruin their attitude for the day.

One important responsibility of a manager is to have an inventory and ordering process in place that gets the tools to a team on time and at the right time. If managers have to justify purchases and investments, then they also need to possess a strong financial understanding of the company's profits and losses and be willing to lay out a good business plan or proposition. It also helps for managers to be passionate and demanding to get team members what they need to deliver results.

One of the many qualities admired in Michael Eisner, the former CEO of Disney, was his ability to divvy up funds for the many projects that his executives brought to him. Hundreds of projects were placed in front of him every year, yet only a couple would ever come to fruition. When it came time to make a difficult decision, he often placed a great deal of emphasis on the passion displayed by the executive presenting the idea. He said, "A strong [point of view] is worth at least 80 IQ points."[19] To get a team the tools to do the job, managers must have strong financial acumen, a thorough and consistent inventory and ordering process, and the conviction that the tools are necessary.

The Right Information

To enable a team, managers must also ensure their people have the right information to do their jobs. In the past, management often was defined by the amount of information people could access. Managers used to maintain control by withholding information. Doing this allowed many mediocre managers to justify their jobs and many enterprising employees to be wasted. A true leader is not threatened by associates who have enough information to be both able and authorized to make decisions. To enable staff members, give them information. Jan Carlzon, CEO of SAS Airlines, wrote, "An individual without information cannot take responsibility. An individual who is given information cannot help but take responsibility."[20]

Providing your people with the right information need not be a major production. We recently worked with a small retail store where the manager could not ensure she would see her people all the time. She set up a clipboard in a central location that contained any relevant memorandums, marketing efforts, and promotions. By directing your people to one location for information, you fulfill the task of providing them with the right information but also place some of the responsibility for gathering information on your staff.

So, to enable your people, get them the training, tools, and information to do the job. Then, for your people to perform at their best, get out of the way and let them do what they were hired to do. You need to empower them.

Performance Empowerment

Merriam-Webster defines "to empower" as "to give power to (someone)."[21] To give power to your people, you need to give them control over how work gets done and allow them to make decisions. Despite all the work we put into getting the best people, onboarding them correctly, training them thoroughly, and enabling their performance, we often fail to truly unleash them to perform on their own because, as managers, we just can't give up control and let our people make decisions.

This is especially noticeable for consumers today. Time is extremely important to customers. According to Kate Leggett, a Forrester analyst in 2013, "71% of customers say that valuing their time is the most important thing a company can do to provide them with good service."[22] How can you show a customer you value their time if whenever employees need to do something for the customer, they have to ask for permission or get approval? This is particularly true when things go wrong. According to a report by the social relationship management company Oracle Social Cloud in 2013, 82% of customers said the number one factor that leads to a great customer service experience is having their issues resolved quickly.[23] How is this expected to happen when employees are not allowed to fix customer problems?

The issue is many managers like being in charge; they like to save the day. Yet if they don't take a step back and empower people to do their jobs and tackle challenges and problems themselves, they will frustrate their staff members and never get the most out of them. This means managers will be forever in crisis mode rather than working on improving their business. Instead, we have to get managers out of the way; we have to help them let go, because it is the only way they will achieve amazing results.

Now, no one is suggesting managers abdicate all managerial responsibilities and never get involved in operations, but there does need to be some balance. If managers are too involved *in* the operation or business, generally they are not working enough *on* the operation or business. Working *on* the operation means focusing on the big picture and looking weeks and months out to direct the team and business successfully through any challenges it might face. When managers are in the operation too much, staff members will come to rely on them too much and then will become distressed or frustrated when they are not around.

A manager's job is to support their employees, not to do everything for them. If managers do tasks for their teams or make decisions for them, they help their employees' performance only in the short term, but by teaching team members how to do their own work and make their own decisions, managers empower performance indefinitely.

In some environments, short staffing requires managers to be in the operation more than necessary, but this should not be a permanent situation. When managers are heavily involved in the operation, their management responsibilities often suffer. A good leader knows and prepares for difficult days or weeks well in advance, ensuring the least amount of disruption takes place. A good leader also prepares staff members for challenges by allocating resources as necessary.

Supporting the operation means being there when necessary and continually having a pulse on the business and people but also continually leading it toward desired results and goals. Even when staff members are empowered, managers still must inspect what they expect and get out from behind the desk to spend time observing, assessing, and ensuring that high performance is happening.

Empowerment requires managers to allow staff members to make decisions on day-to-day tasks and situations they face. It requires staff members to feel supported and to feel that their manager and the organization have their backs. Culturally, knowing that you are trusted to make decisions is very powerful. Kevin Ricklefs, senior vice president of talent management for CHG Healthcare Services, said, "As you give employees a voice and autonomy, a leader's role becomes a coach, a facilitator, and a conduit of information. Leaders do not have to be the single decision makers."[24] In the following box we list some important reminders and steps for managers to take to empower their teams to make decisions.

How to Empower Your Team

- Remind yourself that you do not have to make all the decisions. When an associate comes to you asking "What should I do?" be willing to turn the question back on to them and ask them, "What do you think you should do?" Support the decision even if it is not perfect because this response without any correction will enhance their confidence in decision-making tremendously.
- Remind your staff every day that they can make decisions to enhance or turn around a customer experience or improve how they do work.
- Provide training and simulated scenarios to your people about how they would respond or act in certain situations so that they can learn how to make decisions that benefit the customer and the organization.
- Teach your staff to understand financials, specifically the idea of perceived cost (what the customer thinks they are getting) and real cost (what it actually costs you). Usually the two costs are very different and the main reason why you need to utilize products and services from within your business rather than a third-party company. If you give away a service that is normally $100 to a customer, but in parts and labor only costs you $50, the difference between the two costs is $50. If you give away a service from a third-party vendor that costs the guest $100, but costs you $90 then the difference is only $10. It is important to utilize products or services with the greatest difference between perceived and actual costs.

(continued)

(continued)

- Provide guidelines to help socialize your staff in providing financial compensation to customers. Remember, they are only guidelines and not absolutes.
- Be prepared for your staff to give too much away, but rather than getting upset, recognize the effort. If a decision was made that was a win for the customer, but a financial burden for the organization, utilize it as a training tool and help guide your team to better decision making.

Remember, empowering your people does not mean doing so without guidelines, training, or opportunities to practice. We worked with a large luxury hospitality brand on how to ensure staff members did not give away too many free products in their effort to delight customers. One manager discussed how a new employee took it upon himself to give away 20 free drinks to a group that was celebrating a woman's birthday. When the employee was asked why he did this, he said that he was just trying to "wow" the guests. As I explained, the concept was right, but the execution was wrong. In situations like this, it is important for new staff members to have guidelines or examples of how to delight guests. In the example given, offering just the birthday celebrant a free drink would have provided the "wow" but also would have been financially responsible. When introducing empowerment to staff, it is important to provide them with everyday scenarios where they can think about and decide how to impress customers or turn one around. Have your team share their answers and decide as a group on the best one, and why it was the best. This is an excellent way to socialize staff members into making good decisions.

However, the most important thing is that your people are making decisions and that you instill in them the mindset that not making decisions is not acceptable behavior. I remember reading former CEO of ABB Percy Barnevik's "General Principles of Management Behavior," given as guidelines to his staff in his first meeting with them. I offer his principles as your own guide for why empowering your people is the right thing to do.

To take action (and stick out one's neck) and do the right things is obviously the best. To take action and do the wrong things (within reason and a limited number of times) is second best. Not to take action (and lose opportunities) is the only nonacceptable behavior.[25]

An extension of empowering your people is to provide them with an opportunity and the responsibility for completing some of your managerial tasks. Delegating decisions and tasks will challenge your people to perform up and sets an expectation to continually grow. Remember, if someone else can complete a task 80% as well as you, then you should permanently delegate it to that person. He or she will end up doing it better than you anyway, being focused on this one managerial task, unlike you, who must focus on many.

When I introduced empowerment, I also indicated it was about people feeling they had some control over their work. For people to feel this way, we must engage them to give feedback and ideas about how to improve tasks, positions, and the work being done. This topic is covered in greater detail in Chapter 7 when we discuss how to have your people involved in making improvements to the business.

Managers should be encouraged to not be afraid to give up some of the important tasks that keep them busy every day. Managers become indispensable as leaders when they become dispensable as managers. By empowering and enabling their people, managers not only get them to perform at a higher level but also enable themselves to play better leadership roles.

Establishing the cultural mechanisms and mindset required to achieve the desired performance are important parts of any manager's role and any business's infrastructure. Managers need a clear understanding of what performance is so they can provide feedback on whether their employees are meeting expectations. It is important to see the organization and managers providing their people with the right training, information, and tools. Finally, managers need to establish an expectation around making decisions and provide all staff members with the insights, training, guidelines, and ability to make good decisions. By enabling and empowering your team, you create a culture where your people have the best chance and attitude to meet and exceed your performance expectations.

Culture Hack: Empower and enable your people to maximize their performance.

1. Focus on performance enablement and empowerment rather than just management. The focus should be to elevate performance, not organize or control it.
2. Establish performance goals for each employee based on the organizations objectives for what is to be achieved and the company values to define how those objectives should be achieved.
3. Develop a training plan that lists specific skills, attitudes, and knowledge needed for each position. Develop a learning map that outlines when training will occur and what is to be mastered.
4. Ensure that your staff have the tools, resources, information, and support needed to perform their role.
5. Delegate tasks and decision making to your staff to enhance performance and ensure growth opportunities. Provide guidelines, training, and the encouragement to make decisions and take on new responsibilities. Develop comfort and confidence in your team by trusting them to do the right thing.

Notes

1. Kevin Kruse, "100 Best Quotes on Leadership," *Forbes*, October 16, 2012. http://www.forbes.com/sites/kevinkruse/2012/10/16/quotes-on-leadership/#16ce8f087106

2. "Management," Merriam-Webster.com. http://www.merriam-webster.com/dictionary/management

3. *Culture Hacker* podcast, 2017. Season 1, Episode 4. On-air talent includes: Michelle Crosby, Shane Green.

4. Paul Blake, "Timeline of the Wells Fargo Accounts Scandal." *ABC News*, November 3, 2016. http://abcnews.go.com/Business/timeline-wells-fargo-accounts-scandal/story?id=42231128

5. "Enable," Merriam-Webster.com. http://www.merriam-webster.com/dictionary/enable

6. Quoted in Kevin Freiberg and Jackie Freiberg, *Nuts!: Southwest Airlines' Crazy Recipe for Business and Personal Success* (New York, NY: Broadway Books, 1996), 311.

7. Charles Duhigg, *The Power of Habit: Why We Do What We Do in Life and Business* (New York, NY: Random House, 2012), p. 130.

8. Christopher Pappas, "Top 10 e-Learning Statistics for 2014 You Need to Know," *eLearning Industry*, December 1, 2013. https://elearningindustry.com/top-10-e-learning-statistics-for-2014-you-need-to-know

9. Beverly Davis and Michelle Summers, "Applying Dale's Cone of Experience to Increase Learning and Retention: A Study of Student Learning in a Foundational Leadership Course," *Qscience Proceedings* 2015, Engineering Leaders Conference 2014, p. 6. http://www.qscience.com/doi/10.5339/qproc.2015.elc2014.6

10. Malcolm Knowles, *Self-Directed Learning* (Chicago, IL: Follet, 1975).

11. Ray Makela, "6 Critical Sales Management Actions to Ensure Sales Training Sticks." *Sales Readiness Blog*, n.d. https://www.salesreadinessgroup.com/blog/bid/393959/6-Critical-Sales-Management-Actions-to-Ensure-Sales-Training-Sticks

12. Josh Bersin, "Building the Borderless and Agile Workplace: Bersin & Associates Predictions for 2012," January 1, 2012. Webinar. http://www.bersin.com/Practice/Detail.aspx?id=15135

13. Peter M. Kressaty, email message to author, November 15, 2016.

14. Nespresso, "About Us: Careers at *Nespresso*," n.d. https://www.careersatnespresso.com/working-at-nespresso/about-us/

15. Jackie Range, "Harness People Power," *Financial Review*, May 31, 2012. http://www.afr.com/business/harness-people-power-20120530-jzcnn

16. Heather R. Huhman, "Train to Retain: 7 Tips for Better Employee Training," *Poll Everywhere*, March 25, 2016. http://www.polleverywhere.com/blog/train-to-retain-7-tips-for-better-employee-training/

17. Nespresso, "My Evolution at *Nespresso*: Set Your Career Goals at *Nespresso*!" n.d. https://www.careersatnespresso.com/meet-our-people/my-evolution-at-nespresso/

18. Nespresso, "Development," n.d. https://www.careersatnespresso.com/working-at-nespresso/development/

19. Quoted in Warren G. Bennis, *Managing the Dream: Reflections on Leadership and Change.* (Boston, MA: Da Capo Press, 2000), p. 59.

20. Jan Carlzon, *Moments of Truth* (New York, NY: Harper Perennial, 1989) p. xv.

21. "Empower," Merriam-Webster.com. http://www.merriam-webster.com/dictionary/empowerment

22. Kate Leggett, "Communication Channel Preferences for Customer Service Are Rapidly Changing. Do You Know What Your Customers Need?" *Forrester Research Inc.*, March 15, 2013. http://blogs.forrester.com/kate_leggett/13-03-15-communication_channel_preferences_for_customer_service_are_rapidly_changing_do_you_know_what_your_cus

23. Oracle Social Cloud, *Social's Shift to Service, Why Customer Service Engagement Is the New Marketing.* n.d. http://www.oracle.com/us/products/shift-to-service-2949449.pdf

24. *Culture Hacker* podcast, 2017. Season 1, Episode 6. On-air talent includes: Kevin Ricklefs, Shane Green.

25. Quoted in James O'Toole, *Leadership A to Z: A Guide for the Appropriately Ambitious,* (San Francisco, CA: Jossey-Bass, 1999), p. 12.

6

Coaching

Giving Feedback, the Most Misunderstood and Poorly Executed Leadership Task

Each person holds so much power within themselves that needs to be let out. Sometimes they just need a little nudge, a little direction, a little support, a little coaching, and the greatest things can happen.
                    Pete Carroll, Seattle Seahawks football coach[1]

INFORMAL AND FORMAL FEEDBACK WHEN delivered correctly energizes your people, their attitudes, and their ability to deliver for you.

In Chapter 5, I wrote about the importance of empowering and enabling staff members by providing them with the right training, tools, and information and the ability to make decisions for themselves. To ensure all employees achieve the desired results for their roles, you must have a culture where consistent and meaningful feedback is expected and delivered. Chapter 5 also introduced the 60/20/20 learning model, whereby 20% of all learning comes from feedback or coaching. I believe feedback or coaching is one of a manager's most important responsibilities in terms of achieving results through the people. Fast Company magazine suggests, "All coaches have one thing in common: it's that they are ruthlessly results-oriented."[2] To truly generate success and elevate your employees' performance, you must ensure that coaching is a part of your company's DNA.

Coaching or giving feedback is also about building better relationships with staff members and positively impacting their attitude and engagement with the company. As leadership author and CEO of Box of Crayons Michael Bungay Stanier said, "Coaching is a powerful leadership behavior that drives culture, and engagement, and has a huge impact on an organization."[3] Many of today's employees also eagerly seek out coaching. Without feedback and coaching, they feel underappreciated and unrecognized for what they do well, and they will continue to frustrate customers and managers by not performing as they could or should. According to an Officevibe Study, 65% of employees would prefer more frequent feedback.[4]

According to the *Merriam-Webster* dictionary, "feedback" is "helpful information or criticism that is given to someone to say what can be done to improve a performance."[5] We see feedback as a process by which information is returned to a person about the outcome of an action, process, or activity. It is important to distinguish between two types of feedback, informal and formal.

Informal feedback is everyday casual conversations regarding how work is being done. Formal feedback is more organized, clearly documented, and saved in an employee's or business's files. Many organizations have a problem with feedback because managers just don't know how to do informal feedback right, which means that a lot of the formal feedback mechanisms, such as annual reviews, recognition awards, and employee disciplinary actions, lack credibility and substance.

Many times when we speak to employees on what they think about their annual reviews, they will say that the things discussed were the first time they had heard about them. When asking employees about the recognition process, they say it is all about whoever is up next. And when asked about discipline, employees will often say it is unfair because they were never aware that what they were doing was wrong until they were pulled into the manager's office. A lack of informal feedback is the reason these important formal mechanisms are not positively impacting the attitude and performance of staff.

Effective Informal Feedback

For informal feedback, the basics are simple: It must be timely, fair, consistent, and balanced. We discuss each of these in detail, but first I want to talk about something just as important when it comes to coaching and giving effective feedback, and that is trust.

The Importance of Trust

When we observe managers providing informal feedback to their people, one thing certainly seems to make a difference, and that is the relationship that exists between the manager and the staffer and, more specifically, the level of trust between them. As Douglas Conant, former CEO of Campbell Soup, suggested:

> Trust gives you the permission to give people direction, get everyone aligned, and give them the energy to go get the job done. Trust enables you to execute with excellence and produce extraordinary results. As you execute with excellence and deliver on your commitments, trust becomes easier to inspire, creating a flywheel of performance.[6]

By having a strong relationship with your people, you will naturally have a greater impact on their attitude and performance. Trust is something that often takes time to build; however, it can be quickly developed when the manager cares for and shows an interest in their people. We will discuss this more in Chapter 13, when we focus in on leadership. The manager's ability to give feedback in a timely, fair, consistent, and balanced manner will quickly lead to the development of this critical sense of trust between staff members and the manager.

Feedback Must Be Timely

"Timely" means the feedback should happen when the performance occurs. For this to happen, managers must be in the operation or working alongside staff members. Although formal feedback is often conducted in an office, informal feedback must happen out from behind the desk and closed doors. In thinking about your company and your managerial style, where does most of the coaching occur? If most managers coach and give feedback from their offices, then they are not being timely and effective in one of their most important roles. Ensure that managers spend time every day out of their offices interacting with their staff members and observing them at work. A phrase often associated with military leaders and great managers is "Inspect what you expect." If you expect your people to perform, then inspect their performance; the best place to do this is alongside them as they work. This is also the best time to give feedback.

When feedback is timely, it also can be honest and specific. If a manager provides feedback well after the fact, from other people, or based on hearsay, the accuracy of the feedback can be brought into question. However, if the manager is right there as a behavior is demonstrated or a word is said, the feedback is far more likely to be accurate and usually will be accepted without challenge or distrust. In regards to critiques or feedback about required improvements, it is especially necessary for the information to be given in the moment. When an employee receives feedback about something they need to improve on, then they are far more likely to pay attention to that feedback when it is given in a timely manner.

Feedback Must Be Fair

"Fair" means that you are considerate of the conditions, environment, and what is going on in the moment that a performance occurs. Let's face it, sometimes due to a busy operation, something that is happening to the employee personally, or a lack of training, support, resources, or information, performance will be compromised. As a manager and executive, be considerate of what causes the performance issue to occur. I was told early on in my management career that leaders accept responsibility for the failure of their followers. When it comes to performance and giving feedback, managers must ask themselves if they have done everything to set their employees up for success. If they have, they have met one important condition for effective coaching.

Feedback Must Be Consistent

"Consistent" means managers cannot just give feedback when they feel like it, or at certain times, and only for certain people. There should be no special exception for any employee in your organization, because if an exemption exists, there will be no credibility in your coaching style or feedback. Remember, as US politician Lincoln Chafee said, "Trust is built with consistency."[7] More specifically in the workplace, it occurs through consistent informal feedback.

Feedback Must Be Balanced

"Balanced" means managers provide both positive feedback and feedback for improvement. As managers, we often provide feedback only when something goes wrong because that is what we are trained to do—to be problem solvers, to ensure quality is maintained, and to keep the operation going. Managers seem acutely aware of when things are wrong. As a result, often they are more comfortable pointing out when performance is off or not as expected. Unfortunately, if the only thing staff members hear from their managers is a need for improvement or that things are going wrong, they will slowly start to shut the managers out. It is important for staffers hear a balance of both positive and negative feedback.

However, the idea of balanced feedback goes deeper. In a 2010 article, Ayelet Fishbach, Tal Eyal, and Stacey R. Finkelstein suggested that the need for positive or negative feedback in fact determines on a person's level of expertise in a task or topic. Those who might be considered beginners respond better to positive feedback, while negative feedback can be more effective with experts. According to the article:

> Novices are concerned with evaluating their commitment, and they are more likely to adhere to a goal after receiving positive (versus negative) feedback, in a dynamic of highlighting. In contrast, experts are concerned with monitoring their progress toward the goal and they are more likely to adhere to a goal after receiving negative (versus positive) feedback, in a dynamic of balancing.[8]

As such, a balanced feedback approach must take into account individual differences, as these differences will impact how people respond to what is being said.

Over the years, it has become obvious that many managers are uncomfortable and unable to give credible and confident feedback to their staffers. As a result, it just doesn't happen. Whenever our team at SGEi provide any training on customer service and sales skills or behaviors, first we conduct an informal feedback coaching class to support the training program to be implemented. Without feedback after a training session, the training will have a limited impact at best.

My training team recently implemented an upselling program at the front desk of a large hotel in Las Vegas. The program focused on first impressions, conversations to build relationships, and how to make customized recommendations. We taught these skills over two classes in a three-month period. The outcome of this program was that the front desk was able to generate an additional $2 million in upselling revenues that year, a definite success. However, although the course was great, the real secret to the success of the training was the requirement for all the front desk supervisors and managers to go through an informal feedback class and for every front desk agent to be observed and given feedback on how he or she was doing each week for eight weeks. By teaching managers how to give feedback, we were able to fine-tune the skills we taught in the classroom through coaching. In this program, we applied our 60/20/20 learning rule in a formal and very effective manner.

For any training program to work and for staff members to perform optimally, informal feedback from the manager must occur. The same applies to the implementation of your values. For the values to stick, there must be feedback and coaching on whether your employees are meeting the behavioral expectations of these values or not. Again, when you roll out new values and behaviors to your staff, managers must be ready to provide the necessary feedback. The model in the next section has been successful across many industries and levels of organizations.

The Culture Hacker Informal Feedback Model

We utilize a simple model to teach managers how to give feedback in the operation. The model comes from the Situation-Behavior-Impact (SBI) feedback model, which describes the situation in which the behavior occurred, exactly what the behavior was, why it mattered, and its impact.[9] We have adapted the model to be more interactive. Rather than delivering another lecture, managers should ask employees what the impact of their behavior might be and how they feel they should correct it. In other words, we have to ask questions. In a recent podcast,

Michael Bungay Stanier stated: "The quality of the questions is key to an important coaching session. The best coaching question in the world is 'And what else?' This helps the leader stay curious longer and move to action and advice slower."[10] As a manager, it's vital to learn to ask more questions when giving feedback.

Following is the model we have provided to thousands of managers over the years. Note that this model can be utilized for both positive feedback and feedback for improvement. The method is extremely effective when giving feedback about values or behaviors that are important to the organization. With our model, feedback occurs in five steps. As you will see, there is a focus on asking questions and allowing the employee to provide their own assessment and feedback of the situation.

Informal Feedback Model

1. Give reason for feedback.	"Becky, as you know, one of our habits is to ensure a positive attitude. Do you recall this?"
2. Provide an example of the observed behavior.	"I just listened to your interaction with the last customer, and it did not seem like you were as positive as normal. Did you realize you did this?"
3. Highlight the impact of the behavior.	"What sort of impact do you think that had on the customer?"
4. Was the behavior appropriate? Define next steps.	"How can you ensure you have a more positive attitude with our customers moving forward?"
5. Thank your team member.	"Becky, thanks for supporting our values. Please let me know if you need anything from me to help you with our customers."

By establishing a culture where regular, transparent, and objective feedback occurs, managers will drive performance and positively impact the mindsets of their staffers. This informal feedback also forms the foundation of a meaningful formal feedback program. We want to save the discussion of recognition and counseling for Chapters 8 and 9 but for now, let's address the performance appraisal process, because today it is often the least effective feedback mechanism utilized in organizations.

Effective Formal Feedback

Formal feedback often is epitomized by the annual, dreaded performance appraisal, but it can also be seen in disciplinary action and in official recognition programs. Although formal feedback is important, in many businesses the process has become outdated and stagnant, and it does little to enable or improve team performance. Without informal feedback, formal feedback has little meaning or relevance for team members, so it is important to get the informal feedback going first.

The Performance Appraisal

We have all had that annual review that left us confused, frustrated, or even angry. The annual review in many organizations is merely an annual rite where employees are anxious and managers are underprepared— simply a lose-lose affair. Employees are anxious because the information the review contains is often a surprise, is outdated, and is without foundation. In other words, the review is not based on timely, fair, and consistent informal feedback. Many reviews often fall to the "recency" effect, whereby performance for the entire year is judged on the most recent incidents.[11] Managers are underprepared because the task of remembering an employee's performance over the course of a year and then writing it down daunts them and seems to take too much time. So it's time to rethink the annual review process and programming.

To improve, the annual review needs a makeover, with the formal feedback process becoming clearer, more frequent, and quicker.

Let's begin by making the review clearer. We must start with a clear understanding of what performance is, as we did in Chapter 5. With performance in mind the focus should be on whether employees are meeting their commitments or goals and if they are doing so in line with the values. This assessment is based on those regular informal conversations that are happening.

Next, make these formal conversations more frequent, possibly even every month or two. We are already seeing this shift within organizations as they move away from the traditional annual format and implement regular informal conversations on performance.

The monthly conversations can be kept short by focusing just on those areas where improvement could occur. This conversation does not need to last more than 15 minutes and requires less than a sheet of writing. Many young people seem to prefer this type of casual yet formal feedback, so let's start shifting our perspective and adopting a winning feedback strategy. A quick guide to these monthly conversations follows.

A Guide to the Monthly Performance Recap

- Try to conduct the conversation out of the office and in a comfortable setting.
- With your employees, establish the goal of the conversation, which is to recap any conversations, results, and feedback from the previous month.
- Have employees rate their own performance. Managers should not be the only ones who have to prepare for these important conversations.
- Be honest. There is no value to the leadership or the employees if the feedback is not real and transparent.
- Ask questions about how the employees are feeling and what they are working on in their role to achieve or develop.
- Determine what support you need to provide to help them develop or meet their goals.
- Remember to thank the employees for their contributions, no matter how small.

A large retail group we worked with implemented a monthly feedback program called a leadership assessment. One of the company's values was leadership, establishing an expectation that all staff members had a leadership mentality, regardless of title. Instead of the annual review, each month the managers would sit with their employees individually for 10 to 15 minutes and provide feedback on how they were doing, reviewing key sales statistics, customer feedback, and how they were performing relative to the company values. This formal program ensured that managers and staff were having consistent and relevant conversations.

Technology is having a positive impact in formal feedback. Many companies offer solutions that manage and optimize the formal feedback process, and still more are on the way. Companies like Threads, BetterWorks, Zugata, and Reflektive, to name a few, are transforming the performance review process by making the tasks of documenting feedback, setting goals, and establishing plans more efficient and readily available. Gone are the days when the annual review disappears from sight once given, never to be discussed again.

Although some companies are removing the annual review process completely, for most businesses, the process is not going away. However, by establishing regular monthly check-ins or recaps, the annual review process can become more impactful and meaningful by focusing on goals and plans for achievement. Yes, call them, "Achievement Plans" rather than improvement plans. "Achievement" sounds more positive, and the goal of all managers and coaches should be to help their people achieve something rather than just improve. Mark D. Cannon, a professor of leadership and organizational studies at Vanderbilt University, noted that when feedback is focused on the employee's development, "that makes it a lot more helpful. Feedback becomes a gift of someone investing in the recipient's career."[12] Some guidelines for an effective "Achievement Planning" session are listed next.

A Guide to the Annual/Semiannual Achievement Planning Session

- Schedule for at least an hour, preferably two hours, to allow for in-depth conversations.
- Try to conduct the conversation out of the office and in a comfortable setting.
- With your employees, establish the goal of the conversation, which is again to recap the monthly conversations, but more importantly, to talk about their development and future achievements.
- Have the employees bring their own development plans and needs.
- Ask questions about how the employees are feeling and what they are working on in their role to achieve or develop.
- Remember to thank the employees for being a part of your team and the organization.

Now, the annual review is often tied to incentives and bonuses. I am not advocating that these go away; however, by focusing more on objectives and development in the annual review, bonuses would be tied to how much a person improves and grows rather than whether he or she was "the best." I believe bonuses should be about employees being *their* best, not *the* best. Not only will this shift impact and improve the mindset of all of your people, but it will also improve the performance of a lot more of your staff.

Providing effective feedback through a combination of informal and formal mechanisms is the best way to develop your people to achieve the desired performance and growth. Let's take a look at how Dell uses feedback to enhance employee performance.

Case Study: Dell

Since 1984, Dell has been evolving as a global technology leader.[13] However, in 2012 Dell was struggling to stay afloat in a world where demand for their main product, the personal computer, was quickly declining.[14] A 2013 purchase led to the company becoming private again, thereby shifting the priorities of the leadership team. Shortly after the purchase, Michael Dell enlisted a call to action, stating that the company had to "get out of the destructive cycle of nearsighted decision making and focus on a future that is far beyond the next quarter or fiscal year or election. In this fast-paced, uncertain time, one thing is certain—if we aren't the ones inventing the future, someone else will be.[15]

This call to action meant thinking long-term and putting plans in place to reach their goals. Dell created the 2020 Legacy for Good plan, listing their top priorities and goals. The plan was based on six attributes including a focus on customers, innovation, scaling globally, transparency and accountability, leading by example, and welcoming collaboration. The plan laid out a corporate responsibility framework based on three areas: Environment, People, and Communities.[16] As part of the People plan, leaders were tasked with increasing engagement, team member satisfaction, inspirational leadership, and being recognized as a best-in-class Employer of Choice.[16] To achieve these lofty goals, Dell started by expanding upon their training and development programs to include on-the-job experience and assignments coupled with tailored feedback. Employees are also provided a combination of

(continued)

(*continued*)

networking, coaching, mentoring, and formal learning programs. Targeted external coaching is offered to executives to provide guidance and support to help improve performance and grow leadership capabilities.[17]

Dell transitioned their focus away from the dreaded annual performance review, to providing continuous informal feedback through coaching and mentoring.[18] Managers are encouraged to have frequent conversations with their employees not only about their performance, but also about their personal and professional goals. A 360-degree review process helps to gain performance insights and identify opportunities for growth and improvement. Employees also build networks in which they can give and receive feedback.[17]

Each initiative connects back to the larger 2020 Legacy for Good plan and also to the company's values. Dell continues to progress toward these goals, all the while enhancing their organizational culture. Dell has been recognized for the support of their People, receiving third-party recognition and awards year after year.[19]

If we want our people to be as great as they can be, then, based on our experience, we need to start resetting the mindsets of our managers around the process and idea of performance-based feedback. As Bob Nardelli, CEO of The Home Depot, said perfectly: "I absolutely believe that people, unless coached, never reach their maximum abilities."[20] Your people require managers to be coaches and need a way to get regular, relevant, and meaningful feedback. You and/or your managers must actively provide informal and casual feedback in their operation or work spaces every day, and on this base of casual feedback, more formal feedback is delivered. Think about more regular but less detailed check-ins that build on the annual achievement plans put in place. Any incentives or bonuses are then built around achieving objectives and commitments each year and encouraging all employees to be at *their* best and demonstrate the company values on a daily basis. Commit to being great coaches and enabling your people to be the best they can be through the feedback process.

Culture Hack: Provide effective informal and formal feedback that energizes and develops your people.

1. Coaching requires the delivery of informal and formal feedback.
2. Informal feedback must be timely, fair, consistent, and balanced. It is most effective when there is a high degree of trust between the employee and manager.
3. Informal feedback should involve the manager asking their employee a series of value- and behavior-based questions so they can assess themselves and think about how they can improve their performance.
4. Formal feedback is delivered through a company's recognition program, disciplinary process, and performance appraisal process.
5. The performance review process needs to be updated to include monthly performance recaps and an annual or semiannual achievement planning session.

Notes

1. Jayson Jenks, "Seahawks Coach Pete Carroll Leads Players with Positive Approach," *Seattle Times*, August 29, 2014. http://www.seattletimes .com/sports/seahawks/seahawks-coach-pete-carroll-leads-players-with-positive-approach/

2. Claire Tristram, "Wanna Be a Player? Get a Coach!" *Fast Company*, October 31, 1996. https://www.fastcompany.com/27767/wanna-be-player-get-coach

3. *Culture Hacker* podcast, 2017. Season 1, Episode 3. On-air talent includes: Michael Bungay Stanier, Shane Green.

4. Jeff Fermin, "Statistics on the Importance of Employee Feedback," *Officevibe*, October 7, 2014. https://www.officevibe.com/blog/infographic-employee-feedback

5. "Feedback," Merriam-Webster.com. http://www.merriam-webster.com/dictionary/feedback

6. Quoted in Jennifer Robinson, "Saving Campbell Soup Company," *Gallup Business Journal*, February 11, 2010. http://www.gallup.com/businessjournal/125687/saving-campbell-soup-company.aspx

7. Lincoln Chafee, *Against the Tide: How a Compliant Congress Empowered a Reckless President* (New York City, NY: Macmillan, 2010), p. 201.

8. Ayelet Fishbach, Tal Eyal, and Stacey R. Finkelstein, "How Positive and Negative Feedback Motivate Goal Pursuit." *Social and Personality Psychology*

Compass 4, no. 8 (August 2010): 517–530. https://faculty.chicagobooth.edu/ayelet.fishbach/research/FEF%20Compass%202010.pdf

9. Sloan Weitzel, *Feedback that Works:How to Build and Deliver Your Message* (Greensboro, NC: Center for Creative Leadership, 2000), p. 12-20. https://www.bakersfieldcollege.edu/sites/bakersfieldcollege.edu/files/FeedbackThatWorks.pdf

10. *Culture Hacker* podcast, 2017. Season 1, Episode 3.

11. Mahmoud Javidmehr and Mehrdad Ebrahimpour, "Performance Appraisal Bias and Errors: The Influences and Consequences," *International Journal of Organizational Leadership* 4, no. 3 (2015): 286–302.

12. Quoted in Cynthia M. Phoel, "Feedback that Works," *Harvard Business Review*, April 27, 2009. https://hbr.org/2009/04/feedback-that-works.html

13. Dell Corporation, "About Dell." www.dell.com/about.

14. Ben Worthen and Ian Sherr, "Dell Still Struggling Amid Shift in Computer Market," *Wall Street Journal*, November 15, 2012. http://www.wsj.com/articles/SB10001424127887324735104578121390191628634

15. Michael Dell, "Going Private Is Paying Off for Dell," *Wall Street Journal*, November 24, 2014. http://www.wsj.com/articles/michael-dell-going-private-is-paying-off-for-dell-1416872851.

16. Dell Corporation, "Dell 2020 Legacy of Good Plan." www.dell.com/2020

17. Dell Corporation,"Career Development Programs." http://www.dell.com/learn/us/en/uscorp1/career-development-programs

18. Geoff Colvin, "Microsoft and Dell Are Ditching Employee Performance Reviews." *FORTUNE Magazine*, October 29, 2015. http://fortune.com/2015/10/29/microsoft-dell-performance-reviews/

19. Dell Corporation, "Awards and Recognition." http://www.dell.com/learn/us/en/uscorp1/awards-and-recognition

20. Quoted in Patricia Sellers, "Something to Prove: Bob Nardelli was stunned when Jack Welch told him he'd never run GE. "I want an autopsy!" he demanded," *FORTUNE Magazine*, June 24, 2002. http://archive.fortune.com/magazines/fortune/fortune_archive/2002/06/24/325190/index.htm

7

Strategy, Scores, and Plans

The Real Reason Your People Are Not Engaged

Today, no leader can afford to be indifferent to the challenge of engaging employees in the work of creating the future. Engagement may have been optional in the past, but it's pretty much the whole game today.

Gary Hamel, business consultant[1]

IF YOU ARE GOING TO engage your people and make them responsible for improving your company, then you need to share your objectives and scores, and involve them in the development and execution of plans to achieve those scores.

We have all heard about how important employee engagement is, and as you are reading this book, you are probably thinking that this is what we are really talking about overall. However, let's consider engagement in a more focused way. The *Merriam-Webster* dictionary defines "engagement" as "an arrangement to meet or be present at a particular place and time."[2] The key for me is "to be present", meaning we want our employees to be present at or in their work. Over the years, I have thought a lot about the best way to do this with staff members. I have concluded that having them understand the objectives of the organization, ensuring they know how the company is doing against those objectives, and involving them in achieving those objectives will make people feel they are at the heart of the business and that their presence at work does make a difference. Organizational consultant Warren Bennis provided similar insight when he said, "Good leaders make people feel that they're at the very heart of things, not at the periphery. Everyone feels that he or she makes a difference to the success of the organization. When that happens, people feel centered, and that gives their work meaning."[3]

When you make people feel that what they do matters toward the accomplishment of a great goal, you have engagement. In a 2014 study, Chris Groscurth, a Gallup senior consultant, suggested, "As employees move beyond the basics of employee engagement and view their contribution to the organization more broadly, the more likely they are to stay, take proactive steps to create a safe environment, have higher productivity, and connect with customers to the benefit of the organization."[4] In other words, a sense of purpose has a big impact on the mindsets and attitudes of your people every day.

The idea of people feeling that what they do matters is amplified when dealing with the Millennial generation. Gallup, Inc. sees purpose as one of the most important cultural shifts for many organizations as they deal with their growing Millennial employee base. In a 2016 report, Gallup's chairman and CEO Jim Clifton says, "For millennials, work must have meaning."[5] Although research emphasizes purpose or meaning as being most important with younger workers, the reality is that, throughout history, people have always wanted work that has purpose; it is just that this generation can find purpose more readily. Consider Theodore Roosevelt's 1903 Labor Day speech, where he said, "Far and away the best prize that life offers is the chance to work hard at work worth doing."[6]

Let's face it—everyone would love to feel he or she has a purpose at work. If your employees feel they have purpose in what they do each day or that the organization provides purpose around its efforts in the community or philanthropy it will absolutely have a positive impact on how employees feel about their work. Gallup recognized this in its 2014 study, which indicated that mission and purpose are the two strongest retention factors for Millennials, Generation Xers, and Baby Boomers, so this is truly a multigenerational focus.[7]

Now let's be clear—many organizations have an engagement issue. When we see staff members who are not understanding organizational goals or actively involved in making the organization better, before we blame the staffers, we must consider three important elements. First, we look to see if the company is educating its people on the company goals or objectives. Many times, when we ask staff members, they have no clue about what the organization is trying to achieve. We then look to see if the key metrics around company performance are being shared and discussed on a monthly basis. Often we find scores are just something managers are familiar about and involved with. And then finally, we look to see if employees are expected to and are involved in making plans to achieve those goals or improve those scores. I just do not understand why companies do not involve their people more in making improvements, especially as they usually are the ones with the best ideas. By educating team members on company objectives, updating them on company results, and getting them involved in improvement planning, managers have the ultimate win-win—a more successful company and more engaged team members. Let's consider each in more detail.

Educate Everyone on Company Objectives

Let's start by understanding objectives and what each business should focus on. An objective is simple—it is a goal, something the company aims to reach. I have been involved with many companies across many industries, and my first observation is often that they have too many goals and too much complexity around what they want to achieve. KISS—keep it simple, stupid! Please put that sentence up on the wall during the next annual strategy meeting. As Jack Welch, the former CEO of GE, once said:

> There are only three measurements that tell you nearly everything you need to know about your organization's overall performance: employee engagement, customer satisfaction, and cash flow. It goes without saying that no company, small or large, can win over the long run without energized employees who believe in the mission and understand how to achieve it.[8]

We believe there are four, possibly five, main goals or objectives that you need to focus on regularly, and they line up with what Jack

Welch suggests. When you are setting your objectives, the four that matter most are to:

1. Improve the bottom line.
2. Increase market share.
3. Improve customer satisfaction.
4. Improve employee satisfaction.

Yes, you must have an annual goal around your customer and employee satisfaction. These goals can be measured in a number of ways, but they need to be there. If you are involved in servicing customers, then their feedback matters. If you are committed to ensuring your staff members have the right mindsets and employee experience, then their feedback matters too. I am amazed that so many companies today still fail to make this feedback and satisfaction a priority.

The one other objective to consider is, 'Improve community engagement or social responsibility.' This has become a focus for many companies, especially as it is such an important consideration for our new and younger working generations who want to feel connected to something bigger than themselves. According to Deloitte's 2014 Millennial Report: "Millennials want to leave their mark on the world by working for organizations that benefit society, encourage innovation, and provide them with the opportunity to expand their skills—and they are ready to work independently if their needs are not being met by a traditional organization."[9] Adding an objective to improve the organization's positive impact on society would seem important moving forward.

When you think about your annual objectives, focus on the five basic things to be achieved. These are: improve the bottom line, increase market share, improve customer satisfaction, improve employee satisfaction, and increase community engagement.

Now that the objectives are set, get specific with the number, score, or result that you wish to achieve for each objective. In other words, define the number and measurement that will tell you whether or not you have achieved your goal. Be as specific as possible so that you will know exactly what to aim for and what success looks like. The key here is to have the right measurements in place to keep score. Simply put, if companies are not going to measure their performance against their goals, then they are not serious about achieving desired results. Managers must have a series of objective measurements in place to know how the company is performing. Although many companies measure their financial performance, other goals around market share, customer satisfaction, and employee satisfaction can be vague and a lot more subjective.

Invest in measurement with all of the major shareholders—owners, customers, and employees. In their book *Corporate Culture and Performance*, John Kotter and James Heskett stated, "Firms with cultures that emphasized all the key managerial constituencies (customers, stockholders, and employees) . . . outperformed firms that did not."[10] I am still amazed in today's world at how many customer-oriented companies in hospitality, retail, and entertainment, whose whole reason for being is the customer, have limited measurements and data on how they perform and make their customers feel. When it comes to the customer, no one measurement can define customer satisfaction alone, but online comments must become a part of your customer feedback system.

Your social media reputation—what is being said about you online—is now the most important influencer for customers today, so it makes sense for companies to start paying attention to it. I get it; when running my hotels, I too believed that the feedback on TripAdvisor about my property was just from a bunch of unhappy, inconsequential guests. Today, TripAdvisor is the most influential tool upon which travelers make their hotel reservation decisions. It is the same for every industry; where the customer is talking about you online is where you should be getting information on how you are doing.

When it comes to measurements, you need to ensure that feedback and scores are constantly being received, rather than just at certain times or even once a year. As Mark Sawyier, CEO of Bonfyre, an employee engagement app, said in a recent podcast, "Every company will say that their most important asset is their people, but most companies are asking their people what they think only once a year."[11] We have to stop relying on annual reviews to measure performance or single surveys to understand our customers' satisfaction levels. We need a constant finger on the pulse of how we are performing and how we are doing with our customers and employees, and that means utilizing technology, either your own or a partner's, to give them a forum to speak and a way for you to collect their feedback. I think this feedback outlet is most critical with your staff.

Daniel Espino, vice president of People for the Cosmopolitan, a large hotel in Las Vegas, got it right when he said, "You must give employees a voice and you must be prepared to hear and positively react to what they are saying about your company."[12]

Once you have your objectives and measurements in place, it is important to ensure that staff members understand their importance and impact on the organization. Invest the time to ensure everyone understands what is required and how their role impacts each of the objectives. We discussed in Chapter 5 how important it is to align individual performance with company performance. When objectives are aligned and measurements are understood, it is time to ensure we are sharing the results or scores on a regular basis so that all staff members know how they and the company are doing.

Get and Share Feedback and Results

Once the objectives and measurements have been defined, the next part—sharing the results as they are received—seems easy. However, many employers seem to hesitate to keep their staff up to date with how the company is performing. This outdated thinking hinders the performance of many organizations. If team members don't know the goals or the scores, then how the heck can they be expected to be engaged and responsible for helping to achieve them? Peter Drucker, the famous business consultant, had it right when he wrote, "Management by objective works if you know the objectives: 90% of the time you don't."[13]

So, let's talk about the business buzzword of this decade—transparency. The word transparent means "easy to notice or understand" and to be "honest and open; not secretive."[14] So, when it comes to the company scores, make them easy to understand and not secretive. By having a transparent culture, you make information easily available for the purpose of collaboration, cooperation, and decision making. Remember, it is not just about sharing information. Transparency also requires that staff members can easily see and understand the results.

With transparency in mind, we suggest that the results of the key objectives need to be tabulated into a single scorecard that is easily read and understood by the team. We have developed a number of scorecards for various organizations and provide an example in Figure 7.1. We introduced a similar scorecard to a small company managing

STRATEGIC SCORE	JAN	FEB	MAR	APR	MAY	JUN	JUL	AUG	SEP	OCT	NOV	DEC	TOTAL
Customer Experience													
Customer Survey													
Social Media Reputation													
Associate Experience													
Annual Turnover Rate													
Associate Wellness Survey													
Financial Expectations													
Profitability to Budget													
Market Share													
Market Share													
Community													
Community Service Hours per Associate													
	0	0	0	0	0	0	0	0	0	0	0	0	0

Figure 7.1 Company Scorecard

residential apartments. By making it easy for all staff members to see the scores each month, they became more interested and invested in thinking about how they could make improvements in the day-to-day operations, which, as you will see next, is a critical aspect of employee engagement.

Make sure your scorecard is posted in an easy-to-access place, available in both a soft and hard format. Remember to take the time each month to educate staff members on what each score means and where it is in relation to the annual objectives. Create a culture whereby staff members seek out monthly results to see how they and the organization performed. And remember, be sure the results are shared, no matter if they're good, bad, or ugly.

By sharing key results with staff members, managers can create forthright and honest conversations. This sharing allows managers to involve staff members in the process of improving scores. Technology is making it easier to create strategy, share results, and keep everyone aligned and working toward a shared vision. Companies like Cascade, Envisio, and OnStrategy provide software that aligns the elements of individual and company goals and the supporting action and achievement plans across a company. As Nancy Olsen, cofounder of OnStrategy, suggested, "Good strategy extends beyond leadership teams. When strategy cascades to teams, and individual people see where they fit, how they contribute, and what's expected of them, it creates a powerful alignment throughout an organization."[15]

Get the Team Involved

Once managers are sharing objectives and results, it's time to develop a plan to achieve the goals or improve the scores. Improvement and achievement of the objectives does not happen without a plan. As Antoine de Saint-Exupéry, the author of The Little Prince, wrote, "A goal without a plan is just a wish."[16]

When developing a plan, get out of the office and get the team involved. Educate staff members on the objectives and make them aware of the scores so you can challenge them to come up with ideas about how to improve. Their involvement in developing the plan ensures greater buy-in, better and more relevant ideas from the front line, and more engagement in the business.

When it comes to engaging team members in improvement planning and execution, I teach the following best practice to many organizations:

Strategy to Involve Staff in Business Improvements

- In a department meeting, allow 15 minutes of brainstorming. Remember, there are no bad ideas, so just collect all of the team members' thoughts.
- After the meeting, assign a smaller group of team members, along with the manager, the task of clarifying and prioritizing the ideas. They should focus on ideas that the group and manager can control. They should leave anything not in their control, such as payroll increases, on the list but with a note saying it is something that is not currently actionable.
- Present the updated list back to the team or department, identifying the one or two items that will become the initial focus. Assign participants to teams that will work on developing a more detailed plan and then executing it.
- Write down the plan and update it regularly. Make the plan accessible to everyone on the team and provide progress updates. Consider my Engagement Plan template, shown in Figure 7.2.
- Once changes are implemented successfully, monitor the scores for improvement and adjust as necessary.
- Repeat! Update the priority list with new ideas and focus on the next task to achieve goals.

Our team has introduced and utilized this Engagement Plan template with multiple clients. What makes it my action plan template of choice is that it takes into account all the elements you need to consider if you are serious about making your plans a reality, specifically:

Key Elements for Your Action Plan Template

- Clarity around what objective you are trying to achieve
- The activity you are engaging in to achieve that objective. Recognize that there will be multiple activities to achieve an objective.
- What scores will be used to measure whether or not your activity is a success. Remember if you are not going to measure it, don't bother doing it.

(continued)

(continued)

- All the steps required to complete an activity. I have learned over the years that the more detail given for the steps to be completed, the better chance an activity will be completed.
- Who is responsible for each step to complete an activity.
- The due date for each step to be completed. I am amazed by how many managers operate under plans with no dates for completion.
- What resources, such as time and money, are required to complete a step or activity. Recognize that improvements cost money and by identifying the required investment in your plan it shows you have thought through everything needed to meet your objectives.

I introduced the Engagement Plan template to a group of retailers at one of my workshops. A few weeks later, I received an email from one store manager saying that this template changed his whole management style. He was used to creating lists of to-do items but had never organized them into a format that he could share with both his bosses and his team simultaneously.

Whether you use this template or not, what is important is that your organization bases all action plans on a consistent template so they can be shared easily at all levels of the organization.

Horst Schulze, former president of The Ritz-Carlton Hotel Company, stated, "We make sure our employees know the values, goals, and strategies of our company, because that's the only way they become a part of the company, rather than just coming to work and fulfilling a function."[17] To engage team members, let them in on the worst-kept secret—what the company wants to achieve and how the company is performing each month. When given such information, staffers will not only be more engaged in the business but will also be willing to take on the responsibility of improving every outcome.

Lowe's is a great example of how defining objectives, enlisting proper measurements, and sharing them with employees can lead to desired outcomes.

OBJECTIVE:					
ACTIVITY	SCORES	STEPS	RESPONSIBILITY	DUE DATE	RESOURCES

Figure 7.2 2017 Engagement Plan

Case Study: Lowe's Home Improvement

From the beginning, Lowe's has recognized that the employees are the foundation of their success, providing a competitive advantage that sets them apart from competitors.[18] By focusing on employees, Lowe's experienced significant growth and quality customer care. However, competitors were closing the gap on customer service and the executive team at Lowe's needed to come up with a solid strategy to continue their momentum.[19]

Starting in 2007, Lowe's executive team developed a strategy based on driving employee engagement, as they believed increased engagement would yield to increased performance on other important measures, including customer satisfaction, revenue, safety, and inventory shrinkage. Thus, Lowe's began establishing a data-driven human resources (HR) business model to show causal linkages from HR to business outcomes. The goal was to link HR data, such as engagement surveys, turnover data, sick time, and worker's compensation to marketing, operations, and financial data.[20] In doing so, Lowe's established a data-driven relationship that suggested that higher employee engagement leads to higher sales.[20]

A particularly interesting finding was the relationship between employee engagement, customer satisfaction, and revenue. In particular, the result indicated that engaged employees not only increased customer satisfaction, but also the average ticket price by getting to know the customers and making strategic product recommendations based on their needs. Lowe's estimates that there is at least a $1 million difference in sales between the highest and lowest engaged stores.[20]

Lowe's realized that sharing key measurements with employees was an important part of increasing employee engagement and achieving goals. Constant communication was implemented to connect with employees. Leaders encourage year-round discussions about important metrics and scores and how to get better. Leaders prioritize taking action together with their teams. Employees are encouraged to deliver feedback and submit ideas through Lowe's internal social platform.[21] Training and development programs are implemented to ensure the proper execution of strategy.[21]

In short, achieving company objectives requires the staff to be aware of the key metrics that drive success and be integrally involved in developing plans and completing tasks that improve those scores.

Sharing strategies and scores and then getting your employees involved in the process of achieving those goals or improving those scores is critical for employee engagement and instilling the right mind-set in your organization. When your staff members are present in the moment, understanding how their efforts contribute to the greater good of the organization, they not only feel better but they perform better.

Culture Hack: Get your people engaged and responsible for making positive improvements for the company by sharing objectives and scores and getting them to contribute to a plan.

1. Review annual objectives and goals with each employee to ensure they understand what success looks like.
2. Align individual goals to those of the company.
3. Ensure that results and scores are shared openly with your employees each month. Ensure they understand how the company is doing/ trending to their goals.
4. Make all employees responsible for the achievement of goals and improvement of scores. Host meetings with employees to brainstorm ways to improve.
5. Utilize a common action plan template to document and share what everyone throughout the organization is working on and trying to improve.

Notes

1. Gary Hamel, "Management's Dirty Little Secret." *Wall Street Journal*, December 16, 2009. http://blogs.wsj.com/management/2009/12/16/management%E2%80%99s-dirty-little-secret/
2. "Engagement," Merriam-Webster.com. http://www.merriam-webster.com/dictionary/engagement
3. Warren G. Bennis, *Managing People Is Like Herding Cats* (Philadelphia, PA: Kogan Page, 1998), p. 89.
4. Chris Groscurth, "Why Your Company Must Be Mission-Driven," *Gallup Business Journal*, March 6, 2014. http://www.gallup.com/businessjournal/167633/why-company-mission-driven.aspx
5. Gallup, Inc., *How Millennials Want to Work and Live* (2016), p. 3.
6. Theodore Roosevelt, "Address to the New York State Agricultural Association" (Syracuse, NY: September 7, 1903). Online by Gerhard Peters and John

T. Woolley, *The American Presidency Project.* http://www.presidency.ucsb
.edu/ws/?pid=24504

7. Chris Groscurth, "Why Your Company Must Be Mission-Driven," *Gallup
Business Journal,* March 6, 2014. http://www.gallup.com/businessjournal/
167633/why-company-mission-driven.aspx

8. Quoted in Julie Gebauer and Don Lowman, *Closing the Engagement Gap: How
Great Companies Unlock Employee Potential for Superior Results* (New York,
NY: Penguin, 2008), p. 6.

9. Deloitte Touche Tohmatsu Limited, *Big Demands and High Expectations:
The Deloitte Millennial Survey* (New York, NY: Deloitte Touche Tohmatsu
Limited, 2014), p. 9

10. John P. Kotter and James L. Heskett, *Corporate Culture and Performance*
(New York, NY: Free Press, 2011), p. 11.

11. *Culture Hacker* podcast, 2017. Season 1, Episode 3. On-air talent includes:
Mark Sawyier, Shane Green.

12. *Culture Hacker* podcast, 2017. Season 1, Episode 2. On-air talent includes:
Daniel Espino, Shane Green.

13. Quoted in "Management by Objectives," *The Economist,* October 21, 2009.
http://www.economist.com/node/14299761

14. "Transparent," Merriam-Webster.com. http://www.merriam-webster.com/
dictionary/transparent

15. Nancy Olsen, email message to the author, November 14, 2016.

16. Goodreads, "Quotes by Antoine de Saint-Exupéry." https://www.goodreads
.com/quotes/87476-a-goal-without-a-plan-is-just-a-wish

17. Quoted in Bill Gillette, "Luxury Segment Players," *Lodging Magazine* (October
1998), pp. 54–59.

18. Lowes, "Our Vision and Values." https://www.lowes.com/cd_Our+Vision+
and+Values+Exceptional+Customer+Service_671793447

19. Timothy Thatcher, Benjamin White, and Brian Sutorius, "Strategic Report for
Lowe's Companies, Inc.," Gotham Global, April 18, 2008. http://economics-
files.pomona.edu/jlikens/SeniorSeminars/gotham2007/reports/lowes.pdf

20. Cedric T. Coco, Fiona Jamison, and Heather Black, "Connecting People
Investments and Business Outcomes at Lowe's: Using Value Linkage Analytics to Link Employee Engagement to Business Performance," *People &
Strategy* 34, no. 2 (2011), pp. 28-33. http://c.ymcdn.com/sites/www.hrps.org/
resource/resmgr/p_s_article_preview/ps_34.2_peopleinvestments.pdf

21. Lowe's, "Learning and Development." https://www.lowes.com/cd_Employee+
Engagement+Training+and+Development_655680166

8

Recognition

It's Time to Stop the Meaningless and Mundane Awards Process

There is something that is much more scarce, something finer far, something rarer than ability. It is the ability to recognize ability.

Elbert Hubbard, American writer[1]

THE RECOGNITION PROGRAM IS ONE of the most powerful opportunities managers have to reinforce company culture, improve the mindsets of their people, and improve overall performance. The key is to make the recognition program meaningful, repetitive, and simple.

Whenever I assess a company's recognition program, I simply ask staffers for an honest opinion of how people are selected for awards and recognition. Unfortunately, in many situations, the program that is in place lacks integrity. We are told the recognition is merely a mandated task wherein managers just look for the next person to thank, or recognition is given to those who have been around longest. When this is the case, a great opportunity to positively impact the mindset of your team is lost.

It is not surprising that many employees feel that there is not enough recognition; in fact, in 2014, Kate Taylor, a reporter for Entrepreneur, stated that 82% of staff members feel they do not receive enough recognition.[2] Whether recognition is nonexistent or meaningless, many companies are missing out on one of their best opportunities to positively impact their culture. As former Secretary of Defense Robert S. McNamara suggested, "Brains, like hearts, go where they are appreciated."[3] In other words, your lack of recognition may be one of the biggest reasons why your staff members are leaving you.

What compounds the recognition insanity is that companies are investing a lot of money into their recognition programs every year but getting very little lift in employee attitude or morale. It's time to reinvigorate your recognition program to ensure that it does what it is meant to do—identify those who are performing and reinforce the idea that high performance is good.

As a side note, I find it annoying that so many managers seem reluctant to make a big deal about their best people because they do not want others to feel left out. In today's world, we are raising our children with the idea that everyone contributes and everyone should feel like a winner, but this same idea in the workplace is just reinforcing mediocrity.

The Case for Better Recognition

When we fail to recognize our best people in a consistent and credible manner, we create a dangerous situation around overall performance. Let's say 20% of your team members are superstars and 5% of your people should not be there. This leaves 75% of your staffers somewhere in between and, in some cases, sitting on the fence. That large group of employees will either overperform or underperform, and I believe the choice they make is based largely on what they see happening to the 20% who are superstars and the 5% who are definitely not. Without recognition and accountability—something we talk about in Chapter 9—that 75% of your staffers will underperform, simply because there are no incentives to do well and there are no consequences for doing poorly. Conversely, with recognition and accountability applied, that same 75% will perform up; they may not reach superstar status, but they will certainly perform better than if there were no recognition. The reasoning is very simple—if you or your managers are not recognizing the performance of your best people, then those people will leave, and the 75% of the staff who might aspire to perform at a higher level never will, because there just isn't any incentive to do so.

So, for the sake of your organizational performance, you need to ensure that you are recognizing your best and brightest. This is reinforced by the Aberdeen Group's research report from 2013, which indicated that "60% of Best-in-Class organizations stated that employee recognition is extremely valuable in driving individual performance."[4]

You also have to think about the individuals who receive the recognition; they will have a better mindset about their work and the organization, choosing to stay longer and positively influencing those around them. Bersin & Associates' 2012 research revealed that companies that provide enough employee recognition have 31% lower voluntary turnover rates than companies that don't—a good sign that those employees are happier.[5] Plus, basic psychology indicates that employees who are affirmed for good behavior are more likely to repeat those actions, and that, in the long run, just makes the organization better.

The key to your recognition program is its credibility. As mentioned in Chapter 6, if managers are not providing informal feedback and recognition, then any formal program has very little credibility, so it is important that managers are providing the everyday thanks and high fives. When it comes to employee recognition, a simple verbal or written thank-you is where it all begins. Although many formal recognition programs focus on physical and monetary incentives, the reality is that a simple thank-you is still more meaningful. Also, many small business owners are limited in the amount of rewards they can afford, so focusing on saying thank you and writing it down is the start of any strategy to get staff members thinking positively. Jason Sweigart, a marketing firm owner, says, "Workplace culture has to be positive."[6] Sweigart has found that verbal and written acknowledgments are often worth more than monetary incentives to ensure that positive culture.

When it comes to your culture, begin by ensuring your management teams are actively involved in providing positive feedback, thank-yous, and well-dones in their operations. These simple recognitions are still some of the best motivations to perform and to make your people feel good. Such informal recognition needs to be genuine, in the moment, and based on what is actually seen and heard. As discussed in Chapter 6, this informal recognition must be in place before you focus on any formal system. So just getting all managers to say thank you regularly and with meaning is the first step to making recognition meaningful again.

I am also a big believer in taking the time to write short notes or cards to make this informal recognition stand out. When I was a new manager with The Ritz-Carlton Hotel Company, one of my first bosses instilled in us a habit that, once a week, we would write a thank-you note to one member of our team. It may be a little old-fashioned in today's world of emails, instant messaging, and emojis, but I still believe it is a habit that has meaning. Taking the time to put pen to paper forces you to truly appreciate the people you have working with you, and I believe that those who receive handwritten messages recognize and appreciate the effort.

I also highly recommend taking that recognition beyond the workplace. One week when I was writing my thank-you notes to staff members, I decided to send the notes home. That week we were short staffed and I had to ask a few people to work a lot of long hours. I guess the note was really a thank-you to the families for letting their husband, wife, daughter, or son remain at work so long. In one instance, the worker—a young man who had been in a bit of trouble in the past—came in to my office a few days after his parents had received my note to tell me that his family had celebrated because it was the first time he had received any type of recognition that he made a difference. Sending a thank-you note or recognition to partners, families, or children is a great way to reinforce culture and a sense of relationship. It works, as I found out, and it can really make a difference. The young man just mentioned went on to be a supervisor and excelled in his professional career.

A Meaningful and Lasting Recognition Program

Once you start thinking about a formal recognition program that will involve money and other incentives, there are some simple but important guidelines to follow, which are discussed next.

> **Rules for Your Recognition Program**
>
> 1. Base the Recognition on Performance.
> 2. Recognize the Individual and the Team.
> 3. Offer Rewards the Matter.
> 4. Make Peer to Peer Recognition Easy.
> 5. Be Consistent.

Base the Recognition on Performance

As I indicated at the beginning of the chapter, we have to stop recognizing tenure or just the next person due up. In Chapter 5, we talked about the importance of defining performance clearly throughout the organization. In Chapter 7, we discussed the importance of measurements and being able to align the goals of the company with those of individuals. By basing your recognition on clearly defined performance metrics that are in line with your company's goals you will help ensure your recognition is credible and meaningful. Give formal recognition when company or individual goals are exceeded in a way that is aligned with the values of the organization.

In Chapter 2, we provided you with some example values: creative, collaborative, accountable, and passionate. If these are your company values, it is important that your recognition program recognizes those individuals who meet their commitments in a way that represents these four values. Too many times recognition is given to the person who reaches his or her numbers but does so at the expense of others and without consideration for *how* the person got there. By recognizing people who just hit their numbers, you diminish the importance of your values and disrespect those who try to do things the right way. This problem is common in traditional sales environments, where those who sold the most receive all the focus and recognition, with little consideration for *how* they got those results. By introducing a focus on the values as well as the numbers, I found that people who had not been previously recognized rose to the top. At the same time, employee morale improved, as indicated by their employee satisfaction surveys.

Recognize the Individual and the Team

As discussed, you must recognize your best people, the ones who have performed. If their contribution is recognized, they will be happier and more committed, and it will reinforce their role and importance in the organization. It is also important to recognize team efforts, especially if teamwork and collaboration is an integral part of your values or core culture. Offering a team reward for the achievement of some goal is a great way to promote teamwork. J. W. Marriott, the founder of Marriott Hotels, wrote in his book *The Spirit to Serve* that the best way to develop strong teamwork is to create an environment where the reward of working together outweigh the rewards of individual interests.[7]

One of the best ways to recognize a team is to allow its members to make a presentation to upper management or ownership teams. The opportunity to present and then to receive audible praise as a team is a very effective way to make team members feel appreciated and reinforce the value of working together. In a similar way, bringing in other executives or owners to work areas to provide positive recognition for team efforts is effective and doesn't cost a thing. Another simple and cost-effective reward for team members is to allow them to start an hour late or finish an hour early (obviously dispersing the impact on the operation evenly), or even just giving people an extra 30 minutes for lunch.

Speaking of lunch or meals, consider getting everyone together for a meal, either in or out of work. Cornell University researchers have suggested that teams that eat together perform better together.[8] Bringing your people together for a meal is an excellent form of reward. A large operator of showroom space we worked with implemented monthly lunches with the CEO for teams that performed well every month. Teams were nominated by their managers and had the opportunity to enjoy a meal with the head of the company. The real power of this experience was that staffers could ask the CEO anything they wanted, and soon this event earned the reputation as being something special, because the CEO was willing to be transparent and honest to those in attendance. Not only was it an effective form of recognition, but it also became an important communication mechanism throughout the company, as staff members quickly shared what they learned from the CEO with others.

Teams might also enjoy being involved in a sport or activity outside of work hours. Consider sponsoring such activities as a form of recognition. This form of recognition is particularly effective with young people who seek additional stimulation and workers who are more kinesthetically inclined. When I worked with a private resort in Australia, we made an effort to create social and sporting outlets for the 400-odd staff members. The staff members welcomed the opportunity to participate in sports and activities as recognition for all the work they did. I think the key to this process is to ensure a variety of activities are available so everyone can find something that interests them.

Offer Rewards That Matter

Next, ensure that any program that provides individual rewards offers ones that matter to each individual employee. Know what is important to individuals, whether it's time off with the family, extra money for an upcoming vacation, experiences they might not normally be able to access, or opportunities to grow and be challenged. Everyone is different, so spend some time to learn what each employee values the most. My company has created a simple recognition survey that can be given to staff members to learn how they would like to be recognized and what sort of rewards are most meaningful to them. We encourage managers at other companies to do the same. If the company is small, you can take the time to sit with each person and get to know them and their recognition wish list.

Individual rewards do not need to be just money or things. Think about various ways you can reinforce people's efforts in simple ways, such as with plaques or trophies, letters of commendation in their employee files, some additional time off or breaks, a great parking spot for the month, or even additional responsibilities. An article by Amy Gallo in the *Harvard Business Review* suggested "rely[ing] on intrinsic motivators, such as recognizing contributions, providing opportunities to gain new skills or experiences, and supporting autonomy and choice within a job."[9] Finding ways to recognize high-performing individuals with growth opportunities, which we discuss in Chapter 10, is particularly positive for both individuals and company.

When it comes to things that matter, Millennials have made it clear that charitable contributions are important. A Fortune 500 article by Caroline Preston indicated that two-thirds of people between the ages of 18 and 34 were at least somewhat more likely to want to work for a company that gave to charity than one that did not.[10] Some organizations are now including charitable contributions in their recognition programs, allowing those being recognized to make a donation to their charity of choice in lieu of a personal reward. Goldman Sachs awarded \$175,000 to winners of the Analyst Impact Fund competition, in which teams of analysts around the world competed for a grant for a nonprofit of their choice.[11] Consider how your organization can incorporate charitable donations within your recognition system.

Make Peer-to-Peer Recognition Easy

Create a culture of recognition whereby staff can recognize their peers. Think about it: Why should recognition be left just up to the managers when it is the staff who probably have the greatest insight into who is truly performing at their best. As Michael Levy, CEO of Online Rewards, stated in a recent *Culture Hacker* podcast, "The objective of a recognition program is to keep employees aware of it, engaged in it, and using it. Programs should have a combination of employee-initiated and manager-initiated rewards."[12] A number of recognition tools and software, including Motivosity, Blueboard, Online Rewards, and Kudos, are available that help facilitate this process easily and with integrity. In an article from TINYpulse, an employee engagement software app provider, George Dickson, marketing specialist for a rewards and recognition web platform, states there are some unique benefits of supporting and ensuring that peer recognition happens. He said that doing so is powerful, pertinent, scalable, authentic, inclusive, and educational.[13]

Be Consistent

One final word of advice: Ensure that whatever program you implement is manageable and affordable. In other words, do not create something that could be taken away the moment financial performance stutters. Ensure your program is something that is aligned with company values and is appropriate for the company's bottom line.

We worked with a university administrative group that told us how an inability to be consistent with recognition awards hurt morale significantly. One year the group provided their employee of the year a trip to any US destination. Due to budget constraints, the trip could not be offered the next year. The administration did not announce this fact until the night of the awards. While the winner still received some great compensation, they were still disappointed, the morale of the entire employee group was hurt, and it damaged the reputation of the recognition program. When it comes to recognition, live within your means, and don't underestimate the importance of consistency.

When an organization adheres to these five simple guidelines, recognition truly will make a difference. The next business case highlights how implementing these guidelines can lead to great results, as they have for Southwest Airlines.

Case Study: Southwest Airlines

Southwest Airlines (SWA) is one of the most recognized companies when it comes to employee satisfaction and company culture. Their continued focus on enhancing the employee experience has led to high employee retention (2% voluntary turnover), engagement, and overall company performance.[14] In 2013, SWA unveiled a new corporate vision and purpose, calling their employees to action to make a meaningful difference in the lives of their customers, coworkers, and communities.[15] Southwest employs a multidimensional recognition program that keeps employees striving for excellence and reinforces their culture.

Recognition starts on the ground level with leaders saying thank you to employees on each shift. This simple, yet highly effective habit makes employees feel valued. Daily preshift meetings take place where both individual and team achievements are highlighted.[14] In addition, the Culture Committee hosts frequent events to show appreciation for different departments. For example, Culture Committee members will meet incoming planes, help the flight attendants clean the interior, and provide lunch for the pilots and flight attendants as a way to thank them for their efforts.[16] Employees are also recognized for their tenure by participating in the Annual Awards Banquet for milestone anniversaries.[17]

With more than 46,000 employees at SWA, the leadership team realized that an easy to use, centralized technology platform would be helpful for ongoing employee recognition. Southwest Airlines Gratitude Platform (referred to as SWAG) is a customized platform that allows for centralized recognition and incentive programs.[18] SWAG points are earned from displaying gratitude as a way of life. These points provide a way to appreciate and recognize employees and teams who live the company's values and are high performers. SWAG points can be earned through management or peers, making it easy for everyone to recognize each other on a consistent basis.

(continued)

(continued)
SWAG points provide employees with a common currency that can be exchanged for meaningful awards, including merchandise, gift cards, event tickets, or guest travel passes.[18] Employees who are recognized by customers for their service, are shown appreciation in the company newsletter, intranet, and via a daily video from the CEO shown during preshifts.[14]

Remember that a formal recognition program is one of the best ways to socialize and direct staff members to achieve the desired performance and have the attitude to make a difference. You want to have a recognition program that recognizes *how* work gets done, not just how *much* work gets done. Ensure that any recognition has meaning to the person or team receiving it. Make it easy for staff members to recognize each other and ensure that whatever program you implement can be maintained and funded consistently.

So, make your recognition program meaningful and fun, and don't think it has to involve a large financial spend. As Sam Walton, the founder of Walmart, said, "Appreciate everything your associates do for the business. Nothing else can quite substitute for a few well-chosen, well-timed, sincere words of praise. They're absolutely free and worth a fortune."[19]

Culture Hack: Develop a recognition program that is meaningful, repetitive, and simple to deliver.

1. Recognize those that achieve their goals by adhering to the desired values and behaviors of the company.
2. Managers must informally acknowledge their people with simple thank you's for the formal recognition program to be credible.
3. A verbal or written thank-you is the most powerful and meaningful way to recognize what is being done well.
4. Recognize both the individual and team in such a way that has meaning to them. Provide them with reward options so their recognition matters.
5. Allow employees to recognize each other.

Notes

1. Elbert Hubbard, *A Message to Garcia* (1901), p. 163.

2. Kate Taylor, "Why Do People Actually Quit Their Jobs?" *Entrepreneur*, July 16, 2014. https://www.entrepreneur.com/article/235651

3. Quotes, "Robert S. McNamara." http://www.quotes.net/quote/20943

4. Aberdeen Group, "The Power of Employee Recognition" (November 2013). http://go.globoforce.com/rs/globoforce/images/AberdeenReportNovember 2013.pdf

5. Bersin by Deloitte, "Bersin & Associates Unlocks the Secrets of Effective Employee Recognition," June 12, 2012. https://www.bersin.com/News/Content.aspx?id=15543

6. Quoted in Amy Blackburn, "When Verbal or Written Recognition Works Better than Monetary Rewards," National Association of Sales Professionals. https://www.nasp.com/article/926C0845-E0EE/when-verbal-or-written-recognition-works-better-than-monetary-rewards.html

7. Quoted in Douglas Satterfield, "Core Values: Marriott Hotels," *The Leader Maker*, October 1, 2013. http://www.theleadermaker.com/core-values-marriott-hotels/

8. "Team Building in the Cafeteria," *Harvard Business Review* (December 2015). https://hbr.org/2015/12/team-building-in-the-cafeteria

9. Amy Gallo, "When to Reward Employees with More Responsibility and Money," *Harvard Business Review*, January12, 2011. https://hbr.org/2011/01/when-to-reward-employees-with.html

10. Caroline Preston, "New Poll Shows Millennials Prefer Companies That Give to Charity," *FORTUNE Magazine*, August 11, 2016. http://fortune.com/2016/08/11/millennials-philanthropy/

11. Portia Crowe, "A Bunch of 20-Somethings Convinced Goldman Sachs' Most Senior Staff to Give $200,000 to a Nonprofit," *Business Insider*, June 10, 2016. http://www.businessinsider.com/goldman-sachs-gives-analyst-pitch-competition-2016-6

12. *Culture Hacker* podcast, 2017. Season 1, Episode 4. On-air talent includes: Michael Levy, Shane Green.

13. George Dickson, "6 Unique and Powerful Benefits of Peer Recognition," TINYpulse, June 7, 2016. https://www.tinypulse.com/blog/7-unique-and-powerful-benefits-of-peer-recognition

14. Ken Makovsky, "Behind the Southwest Airlines Culture," *Forbes*, November 21, 2013. http://www.forbes.com/sites/kenmakovsky/2013/11/21/behind-the-southwest-airlines-culture/#4efd0aa83fb9

15. Carmine Gallo, "Southwest Airlines Motivates Its Employees with Purpose Bigger than a Paycheck", January 21, 2014. http://www.forbes.com/sites/carminegallo/2014/01/21/southwest-airlines-motivates-its-employees-with-a-purpose-bigger-than-a-paycheck/#16adcbcf48e1

16. "Southwest Airlines: A Day in the Life of Culture Committee." Online video clip. YouTube, uploaded December 30, 2008. https://www.youtube.com/watch?v=SC1OA5jELTs

17. Southwest, "Work Perks." https://www.southwest.com/html/about-southwest/careers/workperks.html

18. Inspirus, "Southwest: Driving Performance Using Recognition." http://www.inspirus.com/hubfs/Case-Studies/SWA-Case-Study.pdf?t=1445010316405

19. Brian Brinkopf, "Ten Rules of Success from Sam Walton," The Leadership Institute at Harvard College, January 25, 2011. https://harvardleadership.wordpress.com/2011/01/25/ten-rules-of-success-from-sam-walton/

9

Tough Conversations and Decisions

Why We Have People Who Would Be Better Off as Customers than Employees

Executives owe it to the organization and their fellow workers not to tolerate nonperforming people in important jobs.

Peter Drucker, management consultant[1]

ONE OF THE MOST IMPORTANT ways to ensure the overall health of an organization or of individual departments is to hold your people accountable. The key is to do it respectfully and honestly. Although this idea is rarely disputed, the reality is too many managers are not holding poor performers accountable because they are not willing to have tough conversations and make tough decisions.

Due to a lack of accountability, customers are forced to deal with employees who do not give a damn about them or the business. In addition, those employees who don't really want to be there affect the mindset and performance of all those they work with. As I pointed out in Chapter 9, the performance and attitude of many of your staff is

113

dictated by whether there is recognition for your best people and consequences for your worst. I would suggest it is the lack of accountability that is most detrimental to a team or an individual. This seems to be especially prominent when the poor performance is due to a person not doing things the right way or not adhering to the company values.

During my speaking engagements, I often ask the audience to think about the poorest-performing person, the one who is not a good team member, does not meet commitments, or has a consistently bad attitude. When I ask if everyone has one of those people on their team, 99% say yes. Then I ask, "Why the heck are they still with you?" The silence and looks on everyone's faces are priceless. What is even more interesting is that as I go around asking people why, they normally offer a range of excuses, including the union, organizational practices, and even their own culture. What they don't say is that it's really because of them. Now, if I am working with an organization and ask staff members the same questions, almost across the board they will say it's because the manager doesn't hold people accountable. This is the problem: Companies and managers have stopped having tough conversations and making the tough decisions. As a result, employees who should not be there remain in the role long after their expiration date. And by the way, while they remain, some of your best people may leave due to this lack of accountability and action.

Identify Who Needs a Tough Conversation and Who Needs to Go

Let's go back and think about defining performance; in Chapter 5, we indicated that performance should be based on two things—(1) whether employees are able to contribute to the company objectives through their own abilities to deliver the necessary results, and (2) how those results are obtained. You cannot have people achieving required results to the detriment of others. Jack Welch described the idea of performance based on achieving results and sharing values in General Electric's 2000 annual report, where he defined four types of managers.[2] The four types of managers are defined next.

Four Types of Managers

- Type 1: These people deliver on their commitments and share the company values. As we described in Chapter 8, these are the people you have to recognize and reward.
- Type 2: These people are unable to deliver or inconsistent in delivering the required results but have the right mindsets and attitudes that make them a good fit culturally. For these people you should consider investing in their skill development and training to help them get better results. It is important that for these people you place a time limit on how long you will invest in their training and skill development because sometimes you have the right people in the wrong role. There may be another role that better suits their talents.
- Type 3: These people neither achieve the required results nor adhere to the company values. You have to just ask yourself why are they still working with you. While these people are often easy to identify, it is not so easy to understand why they are still working with you. These people must be involved in a disciplinary process that could lead to their termination.
- Type 4: These people deliver on their commitments but are unable to do so without upsetting others or by adhering to your company's values. These people require a tough conversation about the way in which they work. If they cannot improve their work habits, behaviors, or attitude then you must engage in a disciplinary process until they improve or leave the company. These people are the most difficult to manage because they deliver the right results, just in the wrong way. I have seen in many instances where a company or manager has ignored any behavioral or team issues from this person because they need their sales, knowledge, or experience. Unfortunately this focus on deliverables is at the expense of the morale and welfare of other employees around them.

Simply put, of the four types that Jack Welch talked about, two groups require tough conversations and three groups potentially require you to make some tough decisions. Whether we like it or not, as managers, in order to maintain the right culture and ensure the overall success of the organization, we must be able to talk or take action with those employees who are unable to perform.

The next case study highlights the culture of accountability at GE.

Case Study: General Electric

Throughout the years, General Electric (GE) has focused on making progress in all aspects of the business, including culture. It is this relentless focus on improvement that has led to the company's continued success. The culture at GE has evolved, yet the focus on people and accountability remains strong. During his tenure, Jack Welch made it a priority for GE to revitalize the human engine through the transformation of attitudes at GE. He aimed to encourage creativity and feelings of ownership and self-worth.[3]

Performance is based not only on what is accomplished, but also how it is accomplished. As Ragu Krishnamoorthy, vice president of Human Resources at GE Healthcare explains, "The heart of our system has always been about the enormous time commitments the organization and the leadership devote to the conversation about people."[4] Performance management has remained an important part of what makes GE successful. Discussions regarding performance are frequent, thorough, and centered on the company's values.

As Jack Welch stated, "Real communication takes countless hours of eyeball to eyeball, back and forth. It means more listening than talking." Jack Welch held his managers accountable, ensuring they were open, accessible, and straight forward. In his words, "you build the best team, you win."[5] His model is a great tool to consider when determining where your staff or managers fall in regards to performance and maintaining company values.

We have utilized this model in organizations of all sizes and it continues to be a simple and easily adapted model to identify those that need either recognition, training, a tough conversation, or even to be let go.

Having the Tough Conversations

There are many work environments in which people believe that there is no point for formal disciplinary action, because nothing will happen anyway. I have found this attitude in many union environments where managers have become frustrated by their inability to remove truly poor performers. In certain businesses it can be tough to get people terminated but if managers give up on holding people accountable when it is deserved, then not only do they give up one of their important responsibilities as a manager, but they also give up on their people. As I have already indicated, you are more likely than not to have at least one person that should not be with you due to performance issues. And I am betting that as you read this, you are thinking about exactly who they are.

Now, if there is no accountability, then managers are telling the rest of the team that underperforming does not matter and that there are no consequences for bad performance. As mentioned in Chapter 8, a lack of recognition or repercussions sets companies up for bad performance from 75% of the team. The impact this can have on your best and brightest people, those who strive to deliver on the commitments in the right way, is significant, completely frustrating them, demotivating them, and setting them up to leave. Whether you like it or not, without accountability, your people's mindsets will suffer and your customer experience will disappoint.

Well-known speaker Peter Bromberg says, "When we avoid difficult conversations we trade short term discomfort for long term dysfunction."[7] This is a great way to sum up what happens when we fail to hold people accountable—long-term dysfunction. But it does not need to be this way; let's address that short-term discomfort and how to be more confident in formal disciplinary actions.

In January 2002, Beth Axelrod, Helen Handfield-Jones, and Ed Michaels released a study in *Harvard Business Review* of 239 companies that found that high-performing organizations are 33% more likely to take deliberate action against average performers than moderately performing companies.[7] The study found that the number one reason managers did not react to an associate's bad performance is, understandably, an emotional one. We are unwilling to move on people with whom we have worked for a number of years or who have contributed to the company for a long time. The second most common reason was the fear of litigation or having to deal with unions. Other reasons include not knowing what to do, not knowing how to do it, or failing to understand how critical it is to conduct formal disciplinary action. Managing average players is as important in a department's or company's success as selecting and energizing the right players. Holding associates accountable is not about being mean or tough; it's about being relentlessly focused on performance.

So, how do we have tough conversations, and what is the best way to approach employees in need of direction? First of all, check with your human resources department, if you have one, for your rules of engagement. Most companies have a detailed process and forms to be used when giving formal feedback. Each organization is slightly different when it comes to the process, but the most important thing is that there is a process. If you do not have rules of engagement to guide you when having tough conversations, consider using the ones in the next box.

Rules of Engagement for Tough Conversations

- Choose a setting for the conversation that is private and allows for two-way interaction. Think about whether anyone else needs to be involved. Sometimes it is a good idea to have a witness. Other times, another person might have some information or feedback that is essential to the conversation. These conversations don't need to be just between the two of you.
- Be prepared. Come to the meeting ready with key points on what you want to talk about and some real and recent examples of where the employee's performance was not up to standard. Bring solid facts, not opinions. The more objective the conversation, the better.
- Make sure to begin any conversation by reinforcing the team member's value and strengths. Remember: The goal of any conversation is to turn performance around rather than to further erode an already shaky relationship. Always treat underperformers well no matter how much they frustrate you. French leader Napoleon Bonaparte was famous for dealing with poor performers with "an iron hand in a velvet glove."[8] Firmness works better when employed with courtesy and manners.
- Center the discussion around values and seek the team member's input during the conversation. For examples of effective terminology, revisit the Culture Hacker Informal Feedback Model from Chapter 6.
- Form a plan for improved performance over the next 30 days, with specific agreed-on results to be achieved or conditions of improvement to be met. Having a plan at the end of the conversation is key in identifying both what managers are willing to do to enable team member performance and what is to be expected from them in return. The outcomes must be clear.
- Document conversations for the employee's file. Keep a record of conversations so that if the decision to terminate the relationship is made, the company has a history and record of trying to help the employee improve performance.

As we enable our people, we play the role of a coach. In that role, we have to remain focused on what is best for the team and what needs to happen to give the team the best chance to succeed. Although it requires tough love, being a great coach and enabling people is the only way they will get to places they could not have reached alone. American football coach Tom Landry explained, "A coach is someone who tells you what you don't want to hear so that you can see what you don't want to see so that you can be what you've always wanted to be."[9] This is a perfect quote to summarize why these tough conversations are necessary.

Making the Tough Decisions

Now let's talk tough decisions, even though I would argue that the decision should not be that tough if you have done everything you can to set someone up for success and have had the tough conversations. Some people make better customers than they do employees, and there are moments when you should help those employees see that and be that. When I was managing in hospitality, I came across many employees who obviously should not have been interacting with the public. You probably have met them when you have been shopping, dining, calling, or staying at a hotel. Most likely, they are the ones who got into hospitality because it was an easy job and could help pay the bills. The problem was, and still is, many of them stayed even though their hospitality job was meant to be just a short-term gig. When I see employees who obviously do not like serving customers or guests, my first reaction is not to blame them but their managers, the people who are allowing these poor performers to remain in place. The managers are just not willing to make tough decisions.

When it comes to letting someone go, I do not do this lightly, because as a manager, it is important to look at yourself first in such situations. The owner, executive, or manager must ask themselves, "Have I done everything in my power to make that employee successful?" If you are wondering what it means to make an employee successful then this is a perfect moment to think about rereading the first eight chapters. Setting your people up for success means selecting them for both job and cultural fit; orienting and onboarding them correctly;

enabling them with the right training, resources, and information; providing them with fair and consistent coaching; and finally, if they are failing to meet performance expectations, having a series of tough conversations with them. If you feel that you have done all of this, then the decision to let employees go should not be difficult. Remember—firing someone should not be a surprise for either party if you have followed the path laid out in this book and the rules for tough conversations.

Many managers say that the difficulty in letting someone go is often about not wanting to be short-staffed. The thinking is, it is better to have warm bodies, even if they are bad at their jobs, than to have no one. Let me make this clear: This is not better. This is lazy. Not only is having people who frustrate and disappoint customers unacceptable, but the real damage may be happening when they do the same with their co-workers.

There are, of course, emotional considerations, especially when the people you have to fire are those you have known for a long time. There are considerations for them as people and for their families. But remember, in many instances, you may be doing them a favor by forcing them to think about and get a job that better suits their abilities and/or personalities. Remember, Steve Jobs was fired by Apple. In his own words, he said, "It turned out that getting fired from Apple was the best thing that could have ever happened to me. . . . It freed me to enter one of the most creative periods of my life."[10] Of course, he then went back to Apple and, due to this creative period, changed the world.

I think being willing to let someone go is, especially important with young people, a real opportunity for them, even if they are not likely to agree at the time. Do not allow people who are in their first or second jobs to stick around doing something they are obviously not suited for or interested in. As I have said, too many employees stick around in jobs they hate or are not good at. Letting people in their 20s go is a lot easier and more humane than having to let them go in their 40s or 50s.

While emotions are involved in the decision to let someone go, the decision to fire someone should not be an emotional one. Never fire someone on the spur of the moment when you are upset. Firing someone is a serious decision, and it deserves due process and consideration. The decision to let someone go should be based on a series of facts, informal feedback sessions, and conversations. Remember, there are rules in your state about firing someone. Ensure you are following not just your company guidelines but those of your state and all other applicable laws. Readers in the United States can visit the Department of Labor website (www.dol.gov) to review applicable state and federal laws related to termination of employment.

The toughest decision you will have to make is when someone delivers the results you want but unfortunately does so at the expense of peers. However, as we discussed in Chapter 2, your values should act as your guide for these decisions. When you make decisions with your values in mind, you should feel comfortable and confident that you are making the right ones. As reported by the *New York Times*, a Daimler executive was removed after accusations that he had insulted Chinese people during a squabble over parking spots.[11] Regardless of the exact details of the incident, Daimler acted quickly and removed the executive from his role. Why? Well, if you consider that one of Daimler's Guiding Principles is respect and the company states that "economic excellence can only be permanently achieved if the company's actions are aligned with ethical principles that are accepted and perceived to be fair," then you can begin to understand why Daimler made this decision quickly and confidently.[12]

Having worked within the automotive industry, I have seen this situation many times, especially with salespeople who are the dealership's top performers. The top salespeople are allowed to do whatever they want internally, knowing they are safe from being let go because they deliver on or above their sales numbers every month. The decision to let a top performer go is hard; however, almost without exception, when the tough decision was made to remove that salesperson, the overall numbers never dropped, because everyone else on the team performed better and, at the same time, enjoyed coming to work. Removing those whose actions are not aligned with the desired values-based behaviors of the organization may be the toughest decision a manager makes, but when it is in alignment with company values, it is the right decision. I have seen this be one of the most powerful actions to improve company culture or the attitude on a team.

Always show respect and consideration for any employee you are about to let go. Many of the rules we suggest are in place to allow employees to maintain their dignity. The next box presents some simple best practices for when you must let someone go.

Termination Best Practices

- Hold a termination meeting so that letting someone go happens in person—never by email, note, or over the phone.
- Have two people from the company attend, with one person acting as the witness. The witness should be another manager or someone from human resources.
- Conduct the meeting in private and away from other employees. Conduct the meeting at the end of the day, once other staff members have gone, to make the person's exit easier and more private.
- Keep the meeting short, about the facts, and respectful. Ensure you have prepared a detailed list of previous conversations and documentation that has brought both parties to this point. As we have said, your decision should not be a surprise to anyone in the room.
- Have all the logistics worked out. Have the employee's last paycheck ready. Ensure you have a list of the company equipment, identifications, and keys to be returned.
- Ensure the information technology department is in the loop if passwords and access need to be restricted. These restrictions should be put into place before the meeting is concluded. Security might need to be involved in any situation where employees become upset or vengeful. Sometimes dismissed employees must be escorted to collect their personal belongings and out the door, which is why having termination meetings at the end of the day when everyone else is gone has benefits.

When you have let someone go, it is okay to discuss the situation with remaining staff members. Remember to remain positive about the employee who was let go and saddened that it had to come to this. However, letting other employees know that the termination was based on an inability to meet the requirements of the job or to do their job in the right way is an important and powerful message, which I believe can lead to positive improvements in the performance and attitude of others. As Jack Welch said in a 2001 interview after leaving GE, "I was a gardener providing water and other nourishment to our top 750 people. Of course, I had to pull out some weeds, too."[13] And so it is with you: Enable and empower your best people, reward them, and make them better, but understand that along the way, letting a few people go is part of the responsibility of being a good manager and leader.

Paul Foster, CEO and founder of *The Business Therapist*, an online coaching tool said, "Dealing with employee issues can be difficult, but not dealing with them can be worse."[14] Stop being afraid of tough conversations and making difficult decisions about people who do not perform. Successful organizations and managers do both. These tough conversations and decisions are not about emotions, personalities, or bias; they are about being relentlessly focused on the performance of your company and the good of your people.

Culture Hack: Hold your people accountable respectfully and honestly.

1. Don't avoid having difficult conversations or making tough decisions with those that need it because it is uncomfortable.
2. Apply the four types of the managers/staff model to help identify the type of performance plan for each member of your team. Consider what conversations and decisions need to be made.
3. Be willing to have the tough conversations with staff or managers who meet their commitments but fail to do so in such a way that is aligned with your values and aligned with being a good team member.
4. Ensure that you have your own "rules of engagement" that outlines how everyone in the organization should have tough conversations in a professional, respectful, and detailed manner.
5. Be willing to terminate an employee when they continue to perform poorly or not promulgate company values once you have had conversations regarding performance and provided the resources and support to facilitate an improvement.

Notes

1. Peter F. Drucker, "What Makes an Effective Executive," *Harvard Business Review* (June 2004). https://hbr.org/2004/06/what-makes-an-effective-executive

2. General Electric, *GE Annual Report 2000* (February 2001). http://www.ge.com/annual00/download/images/GEannual00.pdf

3. Noel Tichy and Ram Charan, "Speed, Simplicity, Self-Confidence: An Interview with Jack Welch," *Harvard Business Review* (September–October 1989). https://hbr.org/1989/09/speed-simplicity-self-confidence-an-interview-with-jack-welch

4. Raghu Krishnamoorthy, "The Secret Ingredient in GE's Talent-Review System," *Harvard Business Review*, April 17, 2014. https://hbr.org/2014/04/the-secret-ingredient-in-ges-talent-review-system

5. Nadia Goodman, "Jack Welch on How to Manage Employees," *Entrepreneur*, October 5, 2012. https://www.entrepreneur.com/article/224604

6. Peter Bromberg, "Purposeful Influence," Keynote presentation at the Connecticut Library Leadership Institute, West Hartford, CT, August 9, 2013.

7. Beth Axelrod, Helen Handfield-Jones, and Ed Michaels, "A New Game Plan for C Players," *Harvard Business Review* (January 2002). https://hbr.org/2002/01/a-new-game-plan-for-c-players

8. Arthur Lévy, *Napoléon intime* (Nivelles, France: E. Plon, Nourrit et cie, 1893), p. 491.

9. Quoted in Gary Bloom, Claire Castagna, Ellen Moir, and Betsy Warren, *Blended Coaching: Skills and Strategies to Support Principal Development* (Thousand Oaks, CA: Corwin Press, 2005), p. 4.

10. Steve Jobs, Stanford University Commencement Address, Stanford, CA, June 12, 2005. http://news.stanford.edu/2005/06/14/jobs-061505/

11. Chris Buckley, "Daimler Executive Is Removed after Accusations of Insulting Chinese," *New York Times*, November, 22, 2016. http://www.nytimes.com/2016/11/22/world/asia/china-daimler-rainer-gartner.html

12. Daimler.com, "Integrity Code. Common Guiding Principles at Daimler. Our Principles of Behaviour and Guidelines for Ethical Conduct." n.d. https://www.daimler.com/documents/sustainability/integrity/daimler-integritycode.pdf

13. Quoted in Jeffrey E. Garten, "Jack Welch: A Role Model for Today's CEO?" *Bloomberg*, September 10, 2001. https://www.bloomberg.com/news/articles/2001-09-09/jack-welch-a-role-model-for-todays-ceo

14. Paul Foster, "Don't Avoid Firing an Employee," *Business Therapist*, March 12, 2012. http://thebusinesstherapist.com/2012/03/firing-an-employee/

10

Career Development

It's at the Heart of Long-Term Employee Commitment, Yet No One Is Doing Anything about It

It does not matter how slowly you go as long as you do not stop.

Confucius[1]

IT IS TIME TO TALK about career development, a topic on every employee's mind but one that doesn't seem to be as important for many employers. You must have a framework and plan to develop your people and invest in their career.

Let's begin by thinking about what career development means. In his 2010 book *Employee Training and Development*, Raymond A. Noe explains that career development is "the idea of looking at an employee's career as a whole and designing different sets of formal training, developmental activities, and relationships at each stage."[2] In short, career development is about investing in the skills and abilities of your people while providing them with mentoring and coaching for direction. This seems like a very reasonable expectation for today's modern employee, and one that provides a lot of value to the company as well.

It seems over the past couple of years I have been asking employees more and more about their career development aspirations and whether they believe their current company is able to satisfy those needs. The feedback is concerning in that career development just does not seem to be a priority for many organizations today. Yet, with benefits of higher job performance, increased engagement, and lower turnover—all of which positively impact the bottom line, customer satisfaction, and staff mindset—there is a strong business case for investing in career development. So why are companies not focusing on it? Well, based on our conversations with many human resources professionals and business managers, they definitely know of the importance of career development, so there is the talk, but in reality, there's just not a lot of action. A lack of time, resources, planning, and understanding all contribute to companies not investing in one of the more important cultural mechanisms, career development. An old quote says: "When all is said and done, more is said than done." That can apply to many of the ideas we focus on in this book, but it seems to be extremely prevalent in regard to career development.

One concerning attitude that we have come across with managers and small business owners is the belief that there is no point investing in staffers, especially young people, because they are just going to leave anyway. You hear about this a lot, and I think this is a perfect example of a self-fulfilling prophecy, because that lack of investment in an employee's career is probably one of the main reasons they leave you, especially if they are good. And although the cost of investing in staffers who may not stay is significant, consider the cost if they do stay and continue to take care of your customers in a mediocre, disengaged manner. Investing in your employees' careers shows that you care about them beyond just the job, and that care goes a long way toward instilling in your team the right culture and attitudes. Anne M. Mulcahy, the former chair and CEO of Xerox Corporation, put it best when she said: "Employees who believe that management is concerned about them as a whole person—not just an employee—are more productive, more satisfied, more fulfilled. Satisfied employees mean satisfied customers, which leads to profitability."[3]

The Benefits of Investing in the Careers of Your Current Team

Career development is about showing concern for your staff as individuals, but it also has some excellent returns for your business. First of all, it reduces turnover. According to a 2012 Randstad Employee Survey, 86% of employees quit their jobs due to a lack of career development.[4] Turnover is a big expense for many companies, and with younger workers comfortable moving from company to company, any opportunity to keep your best staff and managers a little longer would seem welcome.

An emphasis on career development also encourages people to work harder. Herman Aguinis and Kurt Kraiger's 2009 study in the *Annual Review of Psychology* showed that employees work harder for an organization and stay longer when the organization shows it values the employees by making their career development a priority.[5] Employers like when their employees work harder, so there's another important win for career development.

And, as we discussed in Chapter 7, career development affects employee engagement—the ability to have staff members be and produce in the moment. A report recently released by Career Engagement Group, a career path software company, found that the main reasons for employees choosing to leave their employers were career and job factors, followed by a lack of development and advancement.[6] There's another important reason that career development should be high on your priority list—to help positively influence how your staffers feel about coming to work.

According to Aon Hewitt, a human capital consulting firm, in 2013, the most important driver of engagement was career opportunities.[7] This trend only seems to be becoming more pervasive, with Aon Hewitt stating in 2015 that "career opportunities [are] the number one driver of engagement globally."[8] Aon Hewitt's research in 2013 found that four of the top six engagement drivers were career related.[9] Here are some of the key takeaways from that study:

Key Findings in Aon Hewitt 2013 Research

- Ensure your staff can see clearly how they can grow with you and that development is a priority. People who see this are more likely to be motivated to grow both the business and themselves.
- Give your people opportunities to develop the necessary skills and training to grow not only into their current roles but to also prepare for future roles.
- Managers should take a personal interest in the careers and motivation of staff members.

Next let's consider the role of the organization, manager, and employee, and how they can work together to create a culture positively influenced by career development.

Career Development Must Be Organizationally Supported

Your employees want to develop and grow and this happens quickly and more easily when they know a career is possible. Owners, executives, and managers have a responsibility to ensure that career development is a focus for the organization. In a recent podcast, career expert Anne Fulton said, "By neglecting the career question and not bringing it out, you are taking a massive risk. Pretending it is not an issue is not going to help. Making it open and transparent and having a conversation around it will."[10]

I have often spoken to organizations about this, and I am convinced that many organizations and managers are afraid of career development because they cannot guarantee promotions. However, when you set up paths for promotion, you do not have to promise employees positions in your company. What you are promising is that they will be prepared for promotion either in or outside of your organization. This is important to all staff members but especially to younger people, who want to know right away how you can develop them. Remember, they are comfortable enough to make a jump if a position is not open with you, but you are likely to keep them longer and performing at a higher level by identifying paths to promotion.

So, organizationally, you have to lay out a path for each position in your organization. This path should outline the requirements, experience, and education necessary to excel and achieve a position. By spending time defining the path and performance expectations for each position, you make the process of promotions and development consistent and clear throughout your business.

Next, as an organization, you need to provide training and opportunities to gain experience for staff. This is a significant investment but one that is necessary to keep your best and brightest. This training and experience is particularly important in the development of young managers. I believe that the process of beginning leadership development after people already have a management title is outdated. Think about the damage that could be done while new, and often young, managers try to work out what they should be doing in their new role. Management and leadership training should be offered and available to staff members after they complete their onboarding process. Developing an organization of future leaders may be one of the best ways not only to hold on to your best staff but to improve your customers' experience and the overall organizational performance.

Finally, the organization should support an official mentoring program. We mentioned how this is important for new staff in Chapter 3, but the real benefit comes in guiding career development, particularly in later stages of growth. According to the online talent solution provider Insala in their 2014 Employee Career Development survey report, 17% of respondents believe that mentoring is the most effective method of career development for director level and above, and 36% believe that mentoring is the most effective method for all employees.[11]

Connecting people throughout your organization with seasoned experts in their fields is invaluable for those being mentored, and it also provides mentors with the opportunity to help others. As Gerry Harvey, executive chairman of Harvey Norman Holdings, said, "I get a great deal of joy out of helping people who, over the years, I've spent a lot of time mentoring—and just trying to get them to another level."[12] Reverse mentoring also seems to be gaining prevalence today, whereby young people can provide valuable insights on their Generation Y or Z values, priorities, and what's new with technology.

The bottom line is that mentoring can have a remarkably positive impact on the mindset and loyalty of young people. As US politician Kirsten Gillibrand said, "A strong mentor can help a young woman find and advance in the career of her dreams that otherwise may have seemed impossible."[13]

Career Development Must Be Manager Enabled

Managers must take an interest in the development of their people. This idea is reinforced by Jennifer Robison, a senior editor of the *Gallup Business Journal* in a 2008 article, which found that when someone at work talked to staff members about their progress, the staff members were 92% more likely to stay with the company for another year.[14]

Unfortunately, some managers are so insecure in their own roles and abilities that they focus on keeping staff members in the same roles and places to avoid them showing their ability, instead of trying to make them great. Again, I believe that the only way a manager can become truly indispensable to an organization is to become dispensable—in other words, by developing people to take on the manager's role. Fortunately, because younger workers are so comfortable leaving jobs and managers, we can see more easily which managers are not doing their job of growing talent. Organizations should identify managers who are not creating the right culture for growth and development and consider whether or not they are truly adding value to the business. Think about which managers this might apply to in your own organization.

One method to orient managers toward their career development responsibilities is to make it an expectation and measure on which their performance is assessed. By adding the responsibility of career development to any manager performance program or incentives you orient and influence them to make a difference with their staff.

Career Development Must Be Individually Driven

Entrepreneur Chris Grosser said it best: "Opportunities don't happen, you create them."[15] This should be a reminder to every one of your staff members as they must take responsibility for their own career and its development. For them to do this, the organization must align with their personal values and talents, something we spoke about in Chapter 3 on selection and Chapter 5 on performance.

Although the business and managers play a significant role in creating a culture around career development, employees should be required to show that they want a career and are willing to invest in themselves. To do this, they must take the initiative to seek out the offered training and mentorship opportunities. As you map out paths to achieving promotions or qualifications, ensure you also are requiring employees to engage in personal research, reading, and learning in addition to what the organization is providing to them. Marriott International is a great example of how focusing on career development helps the company align with its value of "We put people first."[16]

Case Study: Marriott International

The hospitality industry has long been plagued with high turnover. In 2015, turnover soared to 72.1% for the industry.[17] However, Marriott has remained a place where employees want to stay and build their careers.[18] Over 10,000 Marriott employees have been at the company for over 20 years, a number many hospitality operators only dream of.[18] Bill Marriott explains that a happy workforce is a cost-saving strategy due to the benefits of having a seasoned staff that know the expectations and are aligned with the company's vision and values.[18] One way Marriott has been able to retain their best people is through delivering on their value of putting people first, which includes an opportunity for employees to grow and advance their careers.

Although there are many perks and benefits provided to Marriott employees, perhaps the most important one is the opportunity for growth and career development. As explained by Daniel Naden, a general manager for one of the properties, "the biggest perk is the opportunity."[18] At the organizational level, continuous training and development is an important piece for all employees. Marriott is often recognized for their extensive training programs, both in-person and through their online portal that offers content in a variety of areas.[19] Marriott's Voyage Global Leadership Development program is designed for new college graduates looking to gain hands-on experience and learn more about leadership before diving into management.[20] All of these

(continued)

(continued)

programs are designed to provide the knowledge and skills needed for employees to advance their careers.

A culture of mentorship and coaching keeps career conversations at the forefront of everyone's minds. A large number of the managers in the company have a history of working their way up from line-level positions. It is made known to all that the opportunity exists for employees to advance their careers; however, employees must put in the time and effort necessary for their own development. Stephanie Linnartz, chief marketing and commercial officer, explains "There's the idea that anyone can make it to the top here if you work really hard."[21]

By implementing a career development program that any person who works hard can be involved in, that managers promote, and that the organization is committed to, you can have a company that people will be happy to remain a part of.

When it comes to career development, Anne Fulton and Jo Mills, authors of *The Career Engagement Game*, recapped my thinking perfectly: "Within your career engagement strategy should be three tiers of initiative at play: Individual empowerment . . . leader enablement . . . [and] organizational effectiveness."[22] When all three elements come together you have a career development framework that will positively impact your employees and how they think and feel about your organization.

Career development is yet another area where technology and software can make a significant difference. Software, such as Fuel 50, Halogen, and Talent Guard, enables employees to take ownership of their careers while providing managers and companies key insights into employee aspirations and fit for the future.

Career development is a critical element of your team's mindset and attitude, and it is only becoming more vital as time goes on. Consider your strategy today, and be prepared to make career development a priority, because your staff already does. You must ensure there is a career development program in place that is organizationally supported, manager enabled, but individually driven.

Culture Hack: Build a framework for developing your people and growing their careers.

1. Invest in the skills and abilities of your people to achieve promotions both inside and outside of your organization.
2. Career conversations must be a priority if you want to retain your best people. It also positively affects job performance and employee engagement.
3. Organizations must provide a career path for each position, detailing the requirements, experience, and education needed to fulfill that role. The organization must offer training programs and opportunities to gain experience in different roles.
4. Managers should be incentivized and recognized when they are able to develop the job skills, managerial responsibilities, and leadership abilities of their people.
5. Provide training and development opportunities whereby the employee can take the initiative and responsibility for their own development.

Notes

1. Confucius and Arthur Waley, *The Analects of Confucius* (New York, NY: Random House, 1938).
2. Raymond A. Noe, *Employee Training and Development*, 6th ed. (New York, NY: McGraw-Hill/Irwin, 2010), p. 297.
3. Quoted in Jim Derivan, "LifeCare, Inc. Conference Features Xerox CEO Anne Mulcahy; Employers Challenged to Motivate and Engage Workforce," *BusinessWire*, May 16, 2003. http://www.businesswire.com/news/home/20030516005369/en/LifeCare-Conference-Features-Xerox-CEO-Anne-Mulcahy
4. Cited in Sharlyn Lauby,"Employees Demand More Career Agility," *HR Bartender*, September 12, 2012. https://www.hrbartender.com/2012/recruiting/employees-demand-more-career-agility/
5. Herman Aguinis and Kurt Kraiger, "Benefits of Training and Development for Individuals and Teams, Organizations, and Society," *Annual Review of Psychology* 60 (2009): 451–474. doi: 10.1146/annurev.psych.60.110707.163505
6. Career Engagement Group white paper, *Hold on Tight—Retention Is Now the Issue: An In-Depth Look at Engagement and Retention in Changing Economic Times* (n.d.), p. 7.

7. Aon Hewitt, *2013 Trends in Global Employee Engagement.* http://www.aon
.com/attachments/human-capital-consulting/2013_Trends_in_Global_
Employee_Engagement_Report.pdf

8. Aon Hewitt, *2015 Trends in Global Employee Engagement: Making Engagement
Happen.* http://www.aon.com/attachments/human-capital-consulting/2015-
Trends-in-Global-Employee-Engagement-Report.pdf

9. Aon Hewitt, *2013 Trends in Global Employee Engagement.*

10. *Culture Hacker* podcast, 2017. Season 1, Episode 5. On-air talent includes:
Anne Fulton, Shane Green.

11. Insala, *Employee Career Development Survey Report*, Arlington, TX: Insala,
2014.

12. Quoted in Ruth Ostrow, "Total Success: For Business and Pleasure, All the
Harveys Need Is Love," *The Australian*, March 1, 2014. http://www
.theaustralian.com.au/life/total-success-for-business-and-pleasure-all-the-
harveys-need-is-love/story-e6frg9zo-1226841082718

13. Kirsten Gillibrand, "Increasing STEM Education for Our Nation's Women,"
Huffington Post, March 21, 2014. http://www.huffingtonpost.com/rep-kirsten-
gillibrand/increasing-stem-education_b_5007171.html

14. Jennifer Robison, "Turning around Employee Turnover," *Gallup Business
Journal*, May 8, 2008. http://www.gallup.com/businessjournal/106912/turning-
around-your-turnover-problem.aspx

15. Quoted in Jonathan Long, "30 Motivational Quotes to Help Realize
Your Entrepreneurial Dreams," *Entrepreneur*, May 7, 2016. https://www
.entrepreneur.com/article/249459

16. Marriott, "Core Values and Heritage." http://www.marriott.com/culture-and-
values/core-values.mi

17. Ron Ruggless, "Hospitality Turnover Rose to 72.1% in 2015," *Nation's
Restaurant News*, March 23, 2016. http://nrn.com/blog/hospitality-turnover-
rose-721-rate-2015

18. Leigh Gallagher, "Why Employees Love Staying at Marriott," *FORTUNE
Magazine*, March 5, 2015. http://fortune.com/2015/03/05/employees-loyalty-
marriott/

19. "HR: Marriott Employee Training and Development Program," *Hotel Management*, June 8, 2010. http://www.hotelmanagement.net/human-resources/
hr-marriott-employee-training-and-development-program

20. Marriott, "The Voyage Global Leadership Development Program."
http://www.marriott.com/careers/paths/entry-level-jobs/hospitality-training-
programs.mi

21. Dan Peltier, "Marriott Uses Its Own Staff to Recruit Employees in New Campaign," October 24, 2014. https://skift.com/2014/10/24/marriott-uses-its-own-staff-to-recruit-employees-in-new-campaign/
22. Anne Fulton and Jo Mills, *The Career Engagement Game—Shaping Careers for an Agile Workforce* (New York, NY: Fuel50 Career Engagement Group, 2014), p. 147.

11

Communication

Why One Size or One Way Doesn't Fit All

Wise men speak because they have something to say; fools because they have to say something.

—Plato, Greek philosopher

COMMUNICATION MAY BE OUR MOST important cultural tool, just as it may be our most important business, leadership, and managerial tool. It is everything and, really, the foundation of many of the mechanisms we have discussed so far. You must be willing to utilize multiple mediums and platforms effectively to ensure your messages are heard and understood. Author John W. Gardner suggested, "If one had to name a single, all-purpose instrument of leadership, it would be communication."[1]

Communication is how any manager or business socializes its employees to understand what is most important and how to be successful while also keeping everyone up to date with what is happening around the office and with the business.

When my team and I begin working with an organization, one of the first cultural mechanisms we test is communication. We look at the various mediums being utilized and spend time talking to front-line staff members about how they are communicated to and what information is shared with them. We also talk to the front-line supervisors who are caught between management and staff—literally between a rock and a hard place. What we often find is too much reliance on emails by managers, boring and ineffective meetings, front-line staffers who have become resigned to a lack of communication, and frustrated front-line managers or supervisors who are just trying to do the best they can to interpret messages and appease staff. Sound familiar? The communication problem in many organizations is severely hurting employees' experience and company culture.

Communication Is All about Understanding

When considering the communication process and programming in your company or department, you have to consider the most important aspect of communication—understanding. To communicate effectively, the audience must understand what is being communicated; otherwise there is no communication. Former CEO of Sovereign Bank (now Santander Bank) Jay Sidhu wrote: "Communication is in the mind of the recipient: you're just making noise if the other person does not hear you."[2]

What does that noise sound like? Well, think about Charlie Brown's teacher, Miss Othmar. Remember what she sounds like? Whenever she talks, it's "Wha, Wha, Wha, Wha, Wha," and this is exactly what managers sound like when team members do not understand the words coming out of their mouths, their emails, or their meetings. As American journalist William H. Whyte once eloquently wrote: "The great enemy of communication . . . is the illusion of it."[3] Unfortunately, many managers seem to be permanently under this illusion.

When it comes to communication through any medium, the focus must be on the recipient's understanding rather than on just sending messages. As American journalist Sidney J. Harris once said, "The two words 'information' and 'communication' are often used interchangeably, but they signify quite different things. Information is giving out; communication is getting through."[4] Often managers and organizations are too focused on giving out messages and information rather than the act of communication.

"Communication" is defined as "the act or process of using words, sounds, signs, or behaviors to express or exchange information."[5] I suggest that the word "exchange" is the most important because communication should go two ways, and it requires a level of understanding from the person being communicated to. As an organization, are you communicating to your staff with the goal of ensuring understanding or just sending out a lot of information?

If communication is mostly about the recipients' understanding, then it is useful to know that people process information differently and, therefore, communication cannot just be delivered in one way. The VAK (visually, auditorily, and kinesthetically) model for learning proposed by Walter Burke Barbe is useful because it allows us to understand how people process information, which is essential to communication. People learn visually, auditorily, or kinesthetically, with one method the predominant way by which they learn and process information.[6] Visual learners prefer seeing or reading to understand, while auditory learners process by listening. Kinesthetic learners learn by experience and doing, and they just happen to be the group we are least effective in communicating to when with lectures. Although it is not likely that you will know each employee's learning preference, knowing the different learning types may help you start to send messages via multiple mediums. Note that we are not saying that you must change your messages; rather you should present them in as many different ways as possible.

It is the responsibility of the manager to check for understanding. When I first became a hotel housekeeping manager, I knew nothing about the department or what good housekeeping entailed. On my second day, my general manager called and asked me to spin the carpet in the front of the house. In my mind, this meant turning the carpet 180 degrees. In the housekeeping world, however, it meant spin bonneting the carpet using a spin bonnet machine. As I knew little about the housekeeping world at the time, I just turned the carpet, literally picking it up and turning it. A few hours later, the general manager called, asking why I had not spun the carpet. I replied I had and got into a short but heated debate, believing I had completed the task. He asked me what I did, and I explained that I had turned the carpet. He began laughing, called me a couple of NSFW words, and then explained what I was meant to do. This example has always stuck with me, and I use it a lot, asking audiences who they believe was at fault in the communication process. Most people believe communication is the responsibility of both parties, which in the normal world is true. However, as a manager, *you* are responsible for the communication process and for ensuring understanding. If communication is done correctly, you would avoid examples like the one I just described.

For communication to be effective in your organization, there needs to be an investment and emphasis by the organization on teaching managers how to use the various mediums available to them correctly and consistently.

Next let us consider all the ways we can communicate our messages efficiently and effectively to our staff and teams.

Communicating Effectively When Speaking

When managers are speaking to staff members, they must remember that just having a title does not necessarily make them effective communicators. Unfortunately, some of the worst speakers use their titles and authority to create the illusion (to themselves) that they are effective. These managers think that their titles mean they can say something once and everyone listening will automatically understand what is meant and will execute on it perfectly. This is a sure-fire way for everyone listening to end up frustrated and confused. Speaking, whether one-on-one or to a group, is a skill, and one that the organization should help their managers develop.

Having researched and delivered many communication training programs over the years, I can provide some important insights into how a manager can speak most effectively to their people to ensure understanding. To begin with, managers must think about keeping their messages short and simple. It is important to get to the point quickly and clearly to promote understanding. I utilize a quote from Winston Churchill, the former UK prime minister, to remind me about the importance of getting to the point. He said, "If you have an important point to make, don't try to be subtle or clever. Use a pile driver. Hit the point once. Then, come back and hit it again. Then hit it a third time—a tremendous whack."[7] So, ensure your managers consider what point they are trying to make and how to deliver it in simple terms. Then remind them that they need to repeat it over and over again to ensure it takes hold.

Regardless of the audience, the timing of when a manager speaks and the environment in which they speak are important considerations. Let's begin with timing. When speaking to staff, either individually or as a group, the time of day matters. Talking to staff in the middle of a busy day or at the end of a day is just not effective; they won't be listening. If managers have something important to say, they should do so when staff members can focus best and avoid distractions, which is usually in the morning or at the beginning of their day or shift. Likewise, where managers speak makes a difference in how communication is received. Speaking to your people in the operation, surrounded by a lot of activity, customers, or noise, is not conducive to effective communication. Communicate in a place where the distractions are at a minimum. As we discuss later in this chapter, preshift meetings are great communication vehicles when managing an operation because they occur before any work begins.

The essential aspect of any verbal communication is actually checking for understanding. If understanding is the goal, then communication must be two way so you can get the necessary feedback to determine whether an understanding has been reached. But please do not think, as many managers do, that by just asking "Do you understand?" the task of communication and checking for understanding is done. As I have learned over the years, many times people answer this question without thinking. As a young manager, I thought I was a great communicator with my 100-plus-person housekeeping team, for many of whom English was the second language, because every time I asked "Do you understand?," I always heard back "Yes." With the accompanying nodding of heads. The reality was only a few understood what I said, relying on those that did to translate after each meeting. I have also seen and heard managers ask their staff to repeat back to them what was just said. Again, this does not really check for understanding, merely an ability to repeat information.

Rather than merely relying on such memorized responses, managers need to be more involved in the communication process and require explanations or demonstrations of what is expected rather than just positive affirmations. Ask staff members to tell you in their own words what they are going to do based on what has been communicated. If time permits, have them demonstrate what they will do. Some staffers told me this was micromanaging; to them I replied, "I call it communication."

Finally, when managers speak, they must believe in what they are saying. Too many times, managers communicate something important without conviction, or their body language and facial expressions contradict what they are saying. Managers lose credibility and believability quickly when the words they speak do not match up with their nonverbal signals.

Dr. Albert Mehrabian, author of *Silent Messages*, conducted several studies on nonverbal communication. His research should be a reminder for every manager, as he found that when communicating, 55% of the message is conveyed through nonverbal cues, such as body language and facial expressions, 38% through the tone of voice, and only 7% from the actual words used.[8]

The idea of nonverbal communication becomes even more important when thinking about your organization's values. Managers are intended to be the champions of the company values, able to explain why those values and behaviors are important and to demonstrate what is expected of each associate. How can a manager expect their staff to buy in to the values of the company if their nonverbal signals don't indicate their own commitment to them? Organizations need to ensure that their managers are able to communicate verbally and nonverbally their commitment to and understanding of the values.

To recap, when managers are speaking, they should keep it short and simple, get to the point, ensure they communicate at a time and in a place that avoids distractions, pay attention to their nonverbal signals and body language, and, finally, check for understanding by asking for explanations or demonstrations.

Communicating Effectively When Writing

Communication often takes place through written notes, notices, and emails. Although the written word is often considered less effective than the spoken word because it mostly fails to communicate emotions and feelings, it is still very important in business today. Remember, visual learners like to process their information by reading and seeing, so a group of your employees will actually prefer to get written messages.

Written messages are extremely important ways to reinforce spoken communication and to communicate facts, data, or scores. However, do not use these written forms of communication, such as emails, in isolation, as some managers might be comfortable doing. All the methods we are discussing must be used in conjunction with other forms of communication.

When writing, managers must ensure that their written communications are grammatically correct and free of spelling errors. With the computer tools and resources now available, error-free communications are easier than ever to deliver. Often mistakes are made when managers are rushing and fail to prioritize grammar. What makes the written form of communication—especially email—so important is that it lasts; in other words, once something is written and sent or delivered, it theoretically does not go away. As email is now the most widely used form of communication in the workplace, managers must recognize the importance of written communications and invest the time to write them correctly.

As far as email is concerned, there is a need in most businesses for some simple etiquette rules to be in place for everyone's sanity and their ability to manage their time. With email now the most popular CYA (Cover your Ass) communication tool, millions of unnecessary emails are sent every day, wasting thousands of hours so a little etiquette could go along way. Consider adopting these rules for everyone utilizing email in your business.

Email Etiquette

- Ensure the subject line is clear about what the email is for. This will allow recipients to manage their priorities and inbox effectively.
- Stop hitting "reply all" unless everyone on the email chain needs to receive your message. And, in case you were wondering, they don't.
- Double-check that you have all the information needed, the correct recipients, and right email addresses before pushing "send." Avoid recalling or resending emails. A simple rule of thumb is to put in the email addresses at the end, after you've written and reviewed the message.

(continued)

(continued)

- Avoid writing in all capitals or using a lot of exclamation points. Writing in all capitals indicates anger or high emotion. Exclamation points convey excitement and attempt to make a point, which is okay, but adding multiple exclamation points to make your point seems immature.
- Don't use email to share or discuss confidential or sensitive information. Make it a rule that if the communication is important, a call or in-person meeting is required.
- Replies to emails should be expected within four hours during a work day; however, there should not be an expectation to reply immediately when someone is at home or on vacation. Culturally, email is creating a conscious or unconscious expectation that people have to respond anytime and anywhere, and this assumption of availability, while possibly not being communicated, is negatively impacting the mindset of many staff and managers.

Although we often wonder how we ever functioned without email, the reality is that it has become one of our biggest challenges in the workplace. As Ryan Holmes, CEO of Hootsuite, a platform for managing social media, suggested, "Email is familiar. It's comfortable. It's easy to use. But it might just be the biggest killer of time and productivity in the office today."[9] With so many emails flying around, many of which are unnecessary, and the expectation of instantaneous responses, we have allowed email to become the biggest disruptor of our day.

When writing, remember to follow many of the same rules we discussed for speaking, keeping it short and simple. Also remember, you still need to check for understanding, so picking up the phone or speaking face to face is still important for those emails and notes to be effective. Also ensure that what is written is grammatically correct and free of errors. Don't be afraid to implement and use some simple email etiquette throughout your company or team. They will be welcomed by everyone.

Communicating Effectively When Doing

The good news is that managers do not have to (and should not) rely on speaking or writing as their only form of communication. Actions speak louder than words, and this is especially true for managers. Remember that the most watched sport in the world is "boss watching." Employees watch the boss for many reasons, but the most important reason is that it is their best way to understand how to act and interact with others. That is why leading by example is a critical communication mechanism.

Keep in mind that setting an example should not just focus on displaying good habits or behaviors with customers, vendors, or other managers; how managers interact and treat the staff is most important. In our *Culture Hacker* podcast, Kevin Ricklefs said, "If we create relationships through honest and open communication, then we set the tone for how our employees should act with our customers."[10] Many times we have heard managers talk about the importance of greeting customers and then have seen them arrive each day and fail to greet their staff members. Managers cannot have the attitude "Do as I say, not as I do." Managers should be examples of the values and behaviors that are the foundation of your company's culture, not the exception. Are your managers fulfilling this important communication role?

We spoke in Chapter 5 about the importance of managers being in the operation to support their staffers. By doing so, managers are able to demonstrate skills and their own mindset about the work to be completed. Remember, many workers learn and process information best by doing, so having managers work alongside staff members and showing them how things should be done can be a powerful communication tool.

Communicating Effectively While Listening

If communication is going to be two way, then we need to talk about listening. Although everyone claims to listen, the reality is, we do not often listen well. Author Nicole Lipkin suggested that "listening is one of the most difficult skills on the planet."[11] Her book, *What Keeps Leaders Up at Night*, outlines some simple exercises for managers to help them listen better and interpret what is really being said to them. To summarize, managers should actually listen, avoiding interruptions or doing other tasks. Listening requires full attention, and staff members deserve it. Managers should listen for emotions and nonverbal cues by acknowledging anything they might be sensing or noticing as their employee talks. Managers should repeat back what was said to them by their employee and ask any clarifying questions to ensure accuracy. Finally, managers should acknowledge what their employee has communicated without criticism.[12] These simple reminders will elevate the communication and relationships within a team.

In terms of building relationships and actually creating opportunities for listening to occur, managers need to be both approachable and available. Although this sounds simple enough, both qualities can be hard to find in the modern workplace.

First, managers need to be approachable, especially when an employee needs to share bad news. Some managers claim that they never receive any bad news from their staff. In these cases, staff members probably have just stopped bringing bad news to them. Some managers are not very good at receiving bad news. In reality, all managers must become comfortable receiving bad news; otherwise, they probably are not getting the important information they need from their staff. To promote the well-being of the culture and mindset of the staff, organizations should train managers in coping mechanisms and habits to help them avoid being emotional and reactive when they receive negative information.

Staff members also need to have access to their managers. Don't say that this is covered by the open-door policy, because that is probably the most disappointing managerial tool mentioned and utilized today. Although most managers are comfortable with staff members bringing them anything, communication at any time is a lot more difficult. When employees ask their manager if they can speak with them, they often hear, "Let's meet later" when it comes to their open-door policy. If there is one thing I have all learned with many managers, it is that "later" never comes.

A best practice in the workplace is for managers to set up times each day when they are truly available, so that staff members can come to rely on actually having communication time when they need it. Outside of emergencies, scheduled open-door times are effective one-on-one communication tools and practices.

If we are committed to a positive and respectful culture, then teaching our managers to listen is an important aspect of communication and leadership. Remind them what author Bryant H. McGill said: "One of the most sincere forms of respect is actually listening to what another has to say."[13]

When it comes to communication, two important mechanisms warrant some further discussion, mainly because they are not being used well or used at all; those mechanisms are meetings and social media.

Communicating Effectively in Meetings

Let's discuss an important communication tool that unfortunately is rendered ineffective too often, and that is the traditional meeting. American author Dave Barry wrote, "If you had to identify, in one word, the reason why the human race has not achieved, and never will achieve, its full potential, that word would be: 'meetings.' "[14] The sad reality is that most employees are likely to agree with Barry.

There are three types of meetings that we should discuss: the daily operations meeting, the weekly update or project meeting, and the monthly departmental meeting. Meetings are important and necessary, but often there are too many of them, and they usually are badly delivered and led.

Daily Meeting

Let's start with the daily meeting. This is generally found in operations and is used to update front-line associates on what is happening or expected to happen during the workday. I believe the daily meeting is the most important communication tool managers have for the front lines. Communication must happen every day, and as we have indicated, one of the important elements that promotes understanding with staff is to ensure the correct timing of the communication and an appropriate environment for it to occur in. By conducting a daily meeting away from customers and other distractions, managers have the perfect opportunity to communicate effectively with staff members. This meeting is an opportunity to share messages, receive feedback, revisit values, and inspire the team in an efficient and effective manner; yet many organizations don't hold daily meetings.

When it comes to the daily meeting, one of the biggest proponents was New York's former mayor, Rudy Giuliani, who wrote: "The morning meeting was the core of my approach to managing."[15] People who have read his book and his description about the events of 9/11 know that he never deviated from his morning meeting even among all the chaos, because he knew that it was his only opportunity to stress priorities and gather information. So, whenever we hear a manager say he or she is too busy to have a daily meeting, Rudy Giuliani comes to mind. If ever there was an excuse not to have a daily meeting, 9/11 was it, but Giuliani never deviated from his meeting schedule.

Here are a couple of points on how to deliver an effective daily meeting for the staff:

Daily Meeting Guidelines

- Keep daily meetings to 10 minutes or less. It is important these meetings do not become long and boring.
- Focus half the meeting on what is happening in and around the operation or business that day. Use the rest for gathering feedback, talking about values and culture, and getting the team ready for the day. The morning meeting should be the switch that ignites the team and reminds them to get to work.
- Get your staff members' attention, and get the staff energized and thinking about what they are about to do for the day. I have seen managers use music or a game, ask questions with a prize for the correct answer, or take their teams to a different part of their business or operation to change things up. As a manager, do not let these daily meetings become predictable.
- Have staff members lead meetings on a rotating basis. Have them come up with creative and fun ways to bring each meeting to life so the responsibility is not always on the manager.

Weekly/Project Meeting

The weekly update or project meeting is called to bring a group of people together to solve problems or to keep managers in the loop. These meetings often become routine and waste time. Common problems are that they may try to cover too many items, are not organized, last more than an hour, have too many people in attendance, involve death by PowerPoint, or just simply lack a purpose. Sound familiar? We thought so. Economist and philosopher Thomas Sowell was quoted in the *Economist* as saying "The least productive people are usually the ones who are most in favor of holding meetings."[16] Let's

The rating is simple; give a 1 for yes and a 0 for no. The output is also simple; useless a meeting scores an 8 or more, it is a waste of the team's time and should be removed or reworked. Here is how to assess a meeting:

Question	Yes	No
Is the purpose of the meeting associated with meeting the company's annual objectives?		
Is there an agenda?		
Are participants asked to review or prepare prior to the meeting?		
Is there a single and clear purpose/topic for the meeting?		
Does it finish within an hour or before the time expected?		
Are there fewer than 10 people involved in the meeting?		
Does the meeting allow all participants to speak and participate?		
Are notes taken and then circulated among the participants after the meeting?		
Are the company values utilized to help direct the decision-making process?		
Does the meeting begin with a recap from the previous meeting and end with the agreed-on next steps and tasks assigned?		
Bouns Question: Does the group often reevaluate whether to meet regularly? (In other words, the meeting should not be about meeting for the sake of meeting.)		
Total		

Figure 11.1   Meeting Scorecard

think about challenging the purpose of and changing the paradigm for these meetings.

Audit regular weekly or project meetings that happen in the organization and rate them on the 11 items measured by the Meeting Scorecard, which is shown in Figure 11.1.

If your meeting does not score at least an 8, begin questioning its relevancy, worth, and ability to make a difference. Use the scorecard as a guide to improving these regular meetings. Remember a project meeting does not need to happen each week; always be willing to meet only as required. Updates and information can be shared via email, utilize meetings to clarify information and make decisions. We have to start limiting the excessive meeting culture that is dominating the workplace and frustrating so many people today.

Monthly Meetings

Monthly department or team meetings have become largely predictable and irrelevant for a number of reasons already mentioned, but they are important and useful communication methods when used properly. We discussed in Chapter 7 the importance of engaging your staff in the planning and execution of achieving goals and improving the business. The monthly meeting is the perfect time to do this.

To make a monthly meeting effective, team members must know that they are expected and encouraged to contribute meaningfully. As a manager, ensure the team's ideas and insights are utilized when prioritizing needs and making decisions. And, as we have already suggested with our weekly meetings, there must be an agenda. We have reviewed a lot of research over the years to ascertain what an ideal monthly meeting looks like, and Figure 11.2 provides an outline.

Learning to implement an agenda and gaining the ability to recap and brainstorm projects and needs for the department can take a bit of time, but once team members understand how they can prepare and contribute, the monthly meeting will become much more efficient and interactive. To help facilitate this process, ensure that each month something from the team's brainstorming list of needs and improvements for the department gets completed so team members can see how their contributions can have a positive impact. To do this managers

TIME	TOPIC
00:00	Welcome and review of agenda.
00:02	Review scores and provide status updates on the work done and information gathered from the last meeting(s). Have someone from the project teams update the rest of the department on progress made.
00:15	Brainstorm on ideas around issues/needs for the team or department.
00:30	Team-building exercise. Include an exercise, game, or discussion that reinforces the company values. This might also involve a guest speaker or a presentation from another team.
00:45	Q&A. Ensure there is an opportunity for two-way interaction on any topic.
00:55	Recognition. Recognize the efforts of individuals or teams.
00:58	A minute of motivation. Have the team walk out energized and excited.

Figure 11.2   Meeting Agenda

should use an action plan, like the one introduced in Chapter 7 to keep track of activities and improvements in the department. Share an updated version of your action plan before or during the department meeting. This will ensure that more people become engaged and excited by the monthly meeting opportunity.

One final reminder: Finish on time. Some companies have best practices in play that utilize a penalty (like having the manager do a push-up for each minute the meeting goes over) to help ensure meetings finish on time. Stick to the schedule and create an expectation with everyone that the monthly meeting always stays on track and on time. For issues that need more discussion, take them off-line or set up a project meeting, as we discussed above, with only those who need to be involved.

Please make meetings relevant and worthwhile. Don't add to the culture and expectation that meetings don't matter—because they do, as long as they are delivered right.

Communicating Effectively via Social Media

Whether we like it or not, and I get that some of you reading this will not, utilizing social media to communicate with your employee base is becoming more and more relevant and effective, especially for younger workers. A Weber Shandwick Study found that 73% of staff would prefer more communication through written means and around 50% want more digital and online communications. Both written and online communication were preferred over face-to-face and telephone communications.[17] We worked with a large retail organization, the majority of whose staff were 22 years of age or younger. As you might expect, they preferred to receive communications via text messaging, so many of the stores implemented an informal group text message system as a way to communicate effectively.

Although there are many fears about how social media will be utilized if it is available during work to all staff and managers, the feedback from organizations we have worked with that have engaged with internal social media platforms suggest that the positives far outweigh the negatives.[18]

When it comes to social media, companies can utilize their own intranet or one of the many excellent third-party platforms available. A social media platform allows staff and managers to engage, discuss, and share ideas quickly and easily. Companies that utilize such platforms have found increased rates of conversations and communication occurring throughout and even across organizational silos. When it comes to selecting your platform of choice, involve your team members, particularly the technologically or social media–savvy ones. They probably already are familiar with many of the sites to be considered. They will also be excellent people to test sites and help in the installation process. Consider them early adopters.

As you consider social media platforms, remember that many young people prefer text messaging because it comes directly to their phones. Whether we like it or not, the smartphone is a key cultural tool of the future. Companies like Bonfyre, HipChat, Slack, and Yammer let you to connect with employees via an app to enable sharing ideas and building relationships. As Mark Sawyier, cofounder and CEO of Bonfyre, said, "If you really want to drive consumption and awareness of the information, it has to be delivered to people's mobile phones."[19]

Although we want to communicate with those staff members who are technologically and socially savvy, let's not forget that a portion of the employee population will not be socially engaged or comfortable online. The Weber Shandwick study mentioned earlier stated that 88% of employees maintain at least one social media site for personal use, but that still means there are 12% who do not.[20] Make sure you engage some of that 12% early to make them comfortable and interested in this new approach. Regardless, and as we have reiterated throughout this chapter, you cannot just rely on one medium for all communication. Although social media seems to be the way forward in company communication, it is still important to build a complete communication strategy that includes a combination of one-on-one meetings, memorandums or notices, emails, meetings, and a social media platform.

When it comes to social media as a communication tool, probably the most important consideration is the commitment of your managers to be active and transparent on whatever platform you choose. Managers also must be comfortable with and ensure that there are no repercussions for staffers who voice any dissenting views or thoughts. You must be willing to invest in making your executives and managers confident in using this communication tool. As SAP president Mike Ettling stated:

> As leaders, you've got to embrace these tools, and use them selectively because they both create significant engagement with your own people and your community. Social media is probably 60 to 70 percent of how we drive thought leadership and awareness in the HR industry today. . . . Good leaders today are using a total multimedia approach to engage and communicate with people.[21]

A great case study for the type of impact a strong internal communication strategy can have is Telstra, Australia's largest telecommunications and media organization.

Case Study: Telstra Australia

Telstra Corporation Limited, known as Telstra, is Australia's largest telecommunications and media company, with over 36,000 employees. Telstra was founded in June 1975 under the Postmaster-General's Department of the Australian government. Located in Melbourne, Telstra serves the entire continent of Australia, with select services available globally. It ranks as one of the largest telecommunications companies worldwide and offers a large range of services to its clients.[22]

As a media provider, Telstra was founded in a highly regulated environment. In the last decade, the industry was deregulated and commercialized, and competition began to pop up. In late 2008, Telstra was known in several market segments for its poor customer service and was losing business to its competition fast. To become viable in the industry again, Telstra had to become more customer-focused and change its culture.

Former CEO David Thodey is widely recognized for his turnaround of the company, starting in 2009. His focus to reinvent Telstra as customer-centric organization not only significantly improved the customer's experience, but also doubled the valuation of the company. He focused on changing the culture at Telstra and is a great advocate of values-based leadership. Thodey said in an Australian *Financial Review* edition, "Our values drive our behavior more than rules, and I think any organization has got to move that way, because it drives people to take ownership and be accountable, and it also

(continued)

(continued)
drives better outcomes for the customer." Telstra utilized their values to transform their culture to a "value service culture," enabling employees to excel at their jobs and provide exceptional customer service.[23]

Thodey realized that to make a significant culture change, he had to influence the attitudes of the employees, develop their skills, and be accessible to hear what employees were saying and make the necessary changes. One of the ways Thodey successfully transformed their corporate culture was through communication and social media.

Telstra is one of the largest users of Yammer, a social network platform that allows companies to share files and data, and to initiate conversations. With more than 25,000 employees registered on the site, Thodey used the forum to comment, communicate, give insights into his thinking, and respond to employee questions and thoughts. Per an article in ZDNet, Thodey suggested that Yammer "has solicited a degree of honesty and openness" throughout the organization. He goes on to say that utilizing this social media platform was "the biggest change in Telstra in terms of breaking down the layers of management and thinking."[24] As Mark Sawyier of Bonfyre said in a recent podcast, "To effectively build relationships, culture, and engagement, a platform is needed for communication."[25]

Telstra has continued to deliver on their value service culture and attributes a large part of the success to the communication and change initiatives that were implemented under Thodey's leadership. As you consider a comprehensive communication strategy, social media must be one of the channels being utilized.

We are just beginning to touch on the potential that digital and social media communication truly have. As Michael Chui, Martin Dewhurst, and Lindsay Pollak noted in a 2013 article in *McKinsey Quarterly*:

There's no doubt organizations have begun to realize significant value from largely external uses of social [technologies]. Yet *internal* applications have barely begun to tap their full potential, even though about two-thirds of social's estimated economic value stems from improved collaboration and communication within enterprises.[26]

When it comes to communication, there is no one-size-fits-all approach. Managers have to engage many mediums to send the same messages to ensure they reach the entire employee audience. Check to see if all your people are receiving the messages being sent and ensure they are being communicated to in the medium they prefer rather than the one you find easiest to manage. Even with multiple communication channels, you still need to ensure messages are understood, so consider how communication is being facilitated throughout your organization and be willing to test to see if all your staff are truly understanding everything that is being said. The most important cultural mechanism in business is communication. Spend the time and money to ensure it is happening clearly and comfortably throughout your company.

Culture Hack: Utilize multiple mediums and platforms to ensure your messages are heard and understood.

1. Communication is a critical cultural tool. You must invest in teaching your owners, executives, and managers to communicate effectively across multiple media and how to ensure understanding.
2. When speaking, ensure the message is short and simple, gets to the point, and is communicated at a time and place that avoids distraction. Always check for understanding by asking for explanations and demonstrations.
3. When using email, follow proper email etiquette such as ensuring correct spelling, an accurate subject line, not hitting reply all to emails unless necessary, and reply in an appropriate amount of time.
4. Leading by example is a key part of communicating for managers. Managers must spend time in the operation in order to demonstrate the expected behaviors.
5. Managers must learn how to listen actively and empathetically. Managers must be approachable and acknowledge when the staff are trying to communicate with them. Managers should schedule time each day where they are truly available so staff can come to rely on having communication time when they need it.
6. Ensure all meetings are relevant and purposeful. Assess the importance of meetings by using a meeting scorecard. Use a meeting agenda in order to be efficient and effective.
7. Consider a social media platform as a great communication tool to connect with younger employees in a way they are comfortable and familiar with using.

Notes

1. John Gardner, *On Leadership* (New York, NY: Simon and Schuster, 1993), p. 166.
2. Pamela Kruger, "A Leader's Journey," *Fast Company*, May 31, 1999. https://www.fastcompany.com/37319/leaders-journey
3. William H. Whyte, "Is Anybody Listening?" *Fortune*, September 1950, p. 174.
4. Quoted in Chris Rose, *How to Win Campaigns: 100 Steps to Success* (New York, NY: Earthscan, 2005), p. 2.
5. "Communication," Merriam-Webster.com. http://www.merriam-webster.com/dictionary/communication
6. Walter Burke Barbe, Raymond H. Swassing, and Michael N. Milone, *Teaching through Modality Strengths: Concepts and Practices* (Columbus, OH: Zaner-Bloser, 1979).
7. Quoted in Virgil Scudder and Ken Scudder, *World Class Communication: How Great CEOs Win with the Public, Shareholders, Employees, and the Media* (Hoboken, NJ: John Wiley & Sons, 2012), p. 120.
8. Albert Mehrabian and Susan Ferris, "Inference of Attitudes from Nonverbal Communication in Two Channels," *Journal of Consulting Psychology* 31, no. 3 (1967): 48-258.
9. Ryan Holmes, "Email Is the New Pony Express—and It's Time to Put It Down," *Fast Company*, October 16, 2012. https://www.fastcompany.com/3002170/email-new-pony-express-and-its-time-put-it-down
10. *Culture Hacker* podcast, 2017. Season 1, Episode 6. On-air talent includes: Kevin Ricklefs, Shane Green.
11. Vivian Giang, "How to Really Listen to Others," *Business Insider*, July 3, 2013. http://www.businessinsider.com/how-to-really-listen-to-others-2013-7
12. Nicole Lipkin, *What Keeps Leaders Up at Night: Recognizing and Resolving Your Most Troubling Management Issues* (New York, NY: AMACOM, 2013).
13. Bryant H. McGill, *Voice of Reason: Speaking to the Great and Good Spirit of Revolution of Mind* (Sarasota, FL: Paper Lyon, 2012), p. 5.
14. Dave Barry, *Dave Barry Turns 50* (New York, NY: Ballantine Books, 1999), p. 183.
15. Rudolph W. Giuliani, *Leadership* (New York, NY: Hyperion, 2002), p. 34.
16. "The Cure for Bad Meetings," Economist.com, n.d. http://transformingbusiness.economist.com/the-cure-for-bad-meetings/
17. Weber Shandwick, "Employees Rising: Seizing the Opportunity in Employee Activism" (n.d.). https://www.webershandwick.com/uploads/news/files/employees-rising-seizing-the-opportunity-in-employee-activism.pdf

18. Paula Berg, "10 Reasons Why You Should Be Using Social Media to Communicate with Employees," *Huffington Post*, February 12, 2013. http://www.huffingtonpost.com/paula-berg/social-media-communicate-employees_b_2666216.html

19. *Culture Hacker* podcast, 2017. Season 1, Episode 3. On-air talent includes: Mark Sawyier, Shane Green.

20. Weber Shandwick, "Employees Rising: Seizing the Opportunity in Employee Activism" (n.d.). https://www.webershandwick.com/uploads/news/files/employees-rising-seizing-the-opportunity-in-employee-activism.pdf

21. Quoted in Danielle Beurteaux, "The Future of Work: Social Media and Employee Engagement," *D!gitalist Magazine by SAP*, May 28, 2015. http://www.digitalistmag.com/future-of-work/2015/05/28/future-of-work-social-medua-employee-engagement-02848959

22. Market Culture, "Telstra Case Study," May 12, 2010. http://www.marketculture.com/downloads/hvc/cases/MarketCulture%20Telstra%20Transformation%20Case%20Study%20-%20May2010.pdf

23. David Ramli and Tony Boyd, "Lessons from David Thodey," *AFR Weekend*, May 1, 2015. http://www.afr.com/leadership/management/decision-making/lessons-from-david-thodey-20150430-1mwzpx–1mwzpx

24. Josh Taylor, "Yammer Breaks Down Telstra's Management Layers," *ZDNet*, June 20, 2013. http://www.zdnet.com/article/yammer-breaks-down-telstras-management-layers/

25. *Culture Hacker* podcast, 2017. Season 1, Episode 3. On-air talent includes: Mark Sawyier, Shane Green.

26. Michael Chui, Martin Dewhurst, and Lindsay Pollak, "Building the Social Enterprise," *McKinsey Quarterly* (November 2013). http://www.mckinsey.com/business-functions/organization/our-insights/building-the-social-enterprise

12

Product, Place, Process, and Perks

The Other Four P's That Define the Employee Experience

Everything from the food employees eat to the technologies they use to get their jobs done to the office spaces they work in are all a part of the employee experience.

Jacob Morgan, Futurist[1]

I HAVE FOCUSED ON THE employee experience throughout this entire book with an emphasis on people; now I want to discuss what I call the other four P's that impact your associates' experience, or how someone feels about coming to work. Now you are probably thinking, I didn't even know there were that many P's to think about, so let me explain.

When considering what creates a customer experience for your company, there are generally four P's discussed: product, place, process, and people. We have been wholly focused on the people element of customer experience in this book. When thinking about the employee experience, we consider five P's: product, place, process, people, and

161

perks. Let's take some time to briefly consider the impact of the other four P's on how your people feel about coming to work every day.

Product

Let's begin with product. The term refers to the item or service you deliver to your customers. Let's face it—some products or services are just better to work on or with than others. We work with a wide variety of companies in multiple industries, and it is clear that at those representing cool, cutting-edge products or services, such as sports teams, fashion, luxury automobiles, or great resorts, employees are more likely to be happy than employees at companies providing less exciting products. But if your company doesn't focus on a product or service that is high on people's desired career list, don't be discouraged. In such situations, the things we have discussed in this book become even more important. Someone has to do the crappy jobs and represent the mundane products or services that, quite honestly, make the world go round. If your company fits this role, the other aspects of the employee experience as described in this book are even more critical.

A word of warning to those people who get to represent cool products or services: Be careful. Do not become complacent—I have seen some instances where the managers and the organization start to think that their people should just be glad they get to work for or with a great product and service, and, therefore, all this other stuff does not matter. Well, it does; you are just lucky enough not to have to overcome a possible disadvantage.

Place

Work areas, back-of-house areas and hallways, break rooms, offices, desks, and anywhere else that employees work or get to take a break are all a part of place. When we talk about place, we want to focus on environment and, more specifically, the environment in which your people work. Environment is defined by your senses. As Immanuel Kant, the famous philosopher, suggested, "That all our knowledge begins with experience there can be no doubt."[2] And so, the sensory experience for your employees plays an important part in how they feel at work.

Let's start with what the employee sees. One of the things that I always look for when visiting various companies is how well they maintain their back of house, employee areas, or places where an employee can take a break. I have a simple philosophy: You cannot expect employees to keep their customer areas immaculate if there is not an effort to do the same for their own areas.

I remember transitioning the Portman Hotel in Shanghai, China to a Ritz Carlton Hotel. This was and still is a, truly beautiful hotel for guests to enjoy. Although the front of the house looked great, in the back of house, garbage was piled up, rats roamed freely, and the place looked like no one cared. This, in fact, was true; the managers had their own restaurant and rest area on one floor that was much more representative of a five-star experience. In the meantime, the rest of the staff were required to walk through, eat, and rest in a very neglected back of house. The first thing we did in the transition was clean up the back of house and require all managers to eat with staff members. Within a day, the food and break room transformed into something special and more in line with what the brand expected. What employees see and touch plays a significant role in their work attitude.

Any employee who works in front of customers, sits at a desk, or must constantly engage in a single task all day must have a place to relax and recharge. I am shocked at the number of high-profile businesses that do not offer anywhere for employees to take a mental and physical time out. We worked with a major convention center where staff worked long hours around thousands of customers and had nowhere to take a break away from those customers. You would see staff members sitting on the floor in hallways, taking breaks in guest areas, or just not getting any breaks. Let me make it clear: You cannot expect employees to be at their best for long periods of time if you cannot provide them with their own space for much-needed time outs. Think about where your employees get to take a break and consider whether the space is conducive to recharging their batteries.

Also, while discussing what people see, consider what posters, information, and even color schemes line the walls in your employee areas. Here is an opportunity to bring employee spaces to life. Or, even better, get staff members involved in painting, placing pictures, and owning the walls in the back-of-house areas or offices. Even just the color of the paint can have a significant impact on how an employee feels at work. Sally Augustin, owner of Design with Science, a cognitive science consultant company, suggested that certain colors evoke similar emotional responses in most people, with green promoting creativity and white leading to boredom.[3]

Color seems particularly important when there is a lack of direct sunlight in a work area. Various research studies have suggested that daylight promotes health and leads to reduced absenteeism, increased productivity, financial savings, and is preferred by workers.[4] In buildings where daylight cannot be integrated, using full-spectrum bright lights has been shown to positively affect the attitude of workers.

What people see should also make them smile. As researchers Bruce J. Avolio, Jane M. Howell, and John J. Sosik suggested, "The use of humor in organizations has been associated with improving morale among workers . . . creating a more positive organizational culture . . . and increasing motivation."[5] I remember walking behind the front desk of a famous luxury hotel and seeing a series of cartoons taped below the lip of the desk where guests could not see them. When I inquired, I was told that the manager placed various cartoons there each day to keep their team smiling, no matter how busy it was. This is a great example of how a manager or organization can remind their people that it is okay to smile.

With regard to what people see and touch, we should also talk about work spaces, areas, and desks. I am not going to get into all the industrial design benefits of certain desks and spaces, but recognize that the design of where your employees work makes a difference in their work habits. There has been a considerable focus on ergonomics, the "science concerned with designing and arranging things people use so that the people and things interact most efficiently and safely" in the workplace.[6] Chairs and desks used at work have been major focuses. As Dr. Alan Hedge, a Cornell University professor of ergonomics, stated, "You don't work on a 1998 computer do you?"[7] Yet the chairs and desks found in many offices today are based on designs for men created more than 70 years ago. Investing in ergonomic chairs and desks improves not only safety and productivity but also how people feel about coming to work. According to Bryan Hornik in Health + Safety magazine, "An ergonomics program in any work environment helps improve employee productivity and morale."[8] This realization is the reason many organizations seem to be investing in providing stunning work spaces for their employees. Employees of these companies with great-looking and highly functional work spaces just seem happier to come to work.

In addition to the design and consideration put into the work space itself, the layout of the space can make a difference with the levels of employee engagement. For example, the use of collaborative work spaces or desks, open and interactive office environments, communal break areas, and spaces to socialize and hang out all foster strong workplace relationships. Why is this important? One popular method of measuring employee engagement is the Gallup Q12 Survey. One of the survey items inquires as to whether or not an employee has a best friend at work.[9] The importance of having a best friend at work reminds us about the importance of workplace relationships. An environment that fosters strong relationships and friendships in the workplace seems to be important for an employees mindset at work. As Mark Sawyier, the CEO of Bonfyre, an employee engagement app software company reminds us, "A huge part of what makes a highly engaged employee is the relationships they have in the workplace, both with their coworkers and the company."[10]

Another important environment element is temperature. In a 2009 poll, Career Builder found that a third of employees had complaints about the temperature of their work space.[11] Research has suggested that the ideal office temperature is 69 to 71 degrees, year round.[12] Any colder or hotter, and your people will be uncomfortable. I know you probably can't make everyone happy, but when was the last time you actually asked your people how the temperature of their work environment felt to them?

We cannot talk about what we see or touch without talking about uniforms, if they are required for your organization. Having a stylish, well-fitting uniform is important, yet it is amazing how many staff members you see in dirty, worn, and, my favorite, too big or too small uniforms. There is no doubt the uniform affects how people feel at work. As Barbara Bell, owner of Bell Uniform Design, said in a discussion with me in 2016, "There's a psychology to great style. In my line of work, I see how people's attitudes, sense of pride and passion for what they do comes alive as they transform their look." Make your employees' uniforms and how they look a priority if you want them to feel good.

With regard to what people hear, plenty of research suggests that certain sounds are more conducive to productivity, but in some ways, this is probably a personal preference. Pay attention to any unnecessary or loud noises. One of the negatives about open work spaces is the excessive noise from others' conversations. According to a report in

Fast Company, Cambridge Sound Management, sound masking experts, found that 30% of employees are distracted by the conversations of their coworkers.[13] Are certain sounds or noises interfering with how your employees feel about coming to work?

The next sense is smell. It should go without saying that bad smells are not going to support a healthy work environment. Although this might seem obvious, I am surprised by the number of businesses that fail to maintain clean employee restrooms, causing some unacceptable smells, not to mention a lack of hygiene. Another consideration occurs when people eat at their desks; the associated food odors can be distracting and offputting to other employees. Think about where certain smells may be distracting or upsetting your staff.

Finally, consider taste. Remember, if you are going to offer beverages, snacks, and even employee meals, you need to do it right. Do not offer food and beverages as a benefit and then deliver poor-quality products. When considering food and beverage options, recognize that many people are much more health conscious today.

In addition to the senses, organizations today need to think about their employee's wellness, something directly tied to their mindset and attitude. With the increased costs of poor health, absenteeism, and a lack of productivity, wellness programs have become an important aspect of any employee experience. Wellness initiatives have mainly focused on fitness-based activities, but have advanced more recently to include lessons in stress recovery, healthy eating, improving sleep habits, and how to unlock the potential of your mind. The focus on wellness seems to pay off. Studies of worksite health promotion programs show that companies that implemented effective wellness programs realized significant cost reductions and financial gains.[14] Studies also suggest that employees who feel their company cares about their well-being are 2.8 times more likely to be extremely engaged.[15] Remember, wellness is more than just access to a gym. By focusing on ways to reduce stress and improve general health, an employee's mindset and attitude will naturally begin to improve.

Process

Next, there is process. In the world of customer experience, process has become extremely important as it considers how well an organization values their customers' time. With a focus on time, companies have started to introduce technologies that make purchases and services more efficient and easier to access. The same consideration needs to apply to your employees. You have to be considerate of their time and make it simple and easy for them to actually be at work.

What do I mean? Well, start by thinking about all the paperwork you require people to fill out when they begin working, when they want to make changes, or when they try to utilize their benefits. Every company seems to have some outdated process that is complicated and frustrates the staff. It's time to address these process shortfalls in your employee experience and show that you value their time, as you should.

Speaking of time, let's talk about flex time. As Rebecca Greenfield stated in *Bloomberg* magazine: "When workers have control over their own schedules, it results in lower levels of stress, psychological distress, burnout, and higher job satisfaction."[16] With the pressures of many working adults to care for family members both young and old, the need to balance both school and work, or the fact that people just want to be more in control of their own time, the willingness of employers to shift from a traditional set schedule seems to create a better mindset and culture. In addition to the opportunity to balance personal and professional responsibilities, companies have started to give their employees the option to work from home more to avoid long commutes, something that can ruin the mindset of even the most positive people. Working from home also allows companies to hire people without traditional geographical limitations, employing people from different cities or even countries to compensate for a lack of talent close by. As serial entrepreneur Kevin Kruse put it:

> The perceived benefits of working from home has [*sic*] enabled me to hire top talent with no local geographic limits. It's enabled me to steal away top talent from competitors, without having to increase their pay. It's contributed to a highly engaged workforce with a company culture that won Best Place to Work awards.[17]

Every company is different, but at the very least, considering flex time or working from home is a credible strategy for a better employee experience.

Perks

Contrary to popular belief, the perks you offer should not be the defining factor for your company's culture, even though when I was consulting with small companies in the Silicon Valley between 2000 and 2002, you would have thought they were. Kegerators, Ping Pong tables, sleeping pods, and nonstop employee events were the norm, and in many companies they remain so today. I am not saying these perks are wrong, because they do have a positive impact on how employees feel about coming to work and it does foster relationships. However, they should not be offered in lieu of the more substantial mechanisms suggested in this book. As Laszlo Bock from Google, one of the companies best known for perks, suggested, "Nurturing the people in your organization doesn't require expensive perks or touchy-feely gimmicks. It's about motivating, engaging and listening—and it can work for anybody."[18]

The following case study on the company DropBox highlights how product, place, process, and perks can affect culture.

Case Study: Dropbox

Dropbox has expanded exponentially since it first came on the technology scene in 2007. Today, hundreds of millions of people rely on the company for file sharing and storage.[19] Despite their rapid growth, Dropbox has remained focused on their fun and quirky culture through providing a great employee experience based on their product, place, process, and perks.

Product: Dropbox has made an incredible difference in how work gets done, for both individuals and companies. To remain competitive, Dropbox invests in innovation and new product development. As stated by product manager Sean Lynch, "We want you to be able to say, 'I know where all my information is—it's in Dropbox. Everywhere I go, whatever device, whatever application, I know that I can pull things out of it."[20] This lofty goal of making Dropbox readily available everywhere keeps employees busy with continual development. Employees are given power and responsibility to grow the company's products, and in doing so, the company has seen immense development.[21] Dropbox has also expanded their products to include collaborative technology, helping teams build upon each other's ideas and work with their latest product, Paper.[22]

Place: Dropbox strives to make their offices personal and magical, no matter how big the company gets. With this in mind, Dropbox offers the ideal environment for collaboration, learning, and recharging. The company strives to provide a place that takes stress out of life and makes coming to work enjoyable.[23]

Process: The company emphasizes work-life balance and provides exceptional health and wellness benefits, as well as a generous time-off policy. Employees can easily access their information through an internal portal, making the process of taking a vacation or enrolling in benefits seamless.[23] They strive to maintain simplicity for both employees and customers. Dropbox does an exceptional job at removing pain points for their employees so that they can focus on their work in a collaborative and energizing environment.

Perks: Dropbox offers employees workout facilities, game rooms, complementary meals, laundry service, and guest speaker sessions as perks for being a part of the team.

The four P's are all important considerations when it comes to the employee experience. There is no right or wrong mix of elements, as long as each is given an appropriate focus.

As you consider your employees' experience, you must consider how the other 4 P's can make a difference. There is no right or wrong combination of P's for your organization, as long as you are considerate of the part they play in your employees' daily work experience. The right mix of P's can elevate the employee experience and positively impact how your people feel about coming to work. Look for opportunities that are easy to implement, inexpensive to offer, and, most importantly, are meaningful for your team. If you want your employee experience to be exceptional, you must be willing to move beyond traditional office elements and work practices.

Culture Hack: Consider the other four P's when critiquing and improving your employee experience.

1. Make employee experience a priority regardless of the product or service your company delivers. However, the less exciting the product, the more emphasis you need to place on ensuring a great experience.
2. Provide an environment that enlivens your employees' senses, provides them with an opportunity to take breaks, and is devoid of annoying distractions.
3. Offer social and collaborative opportunities for your people to get to know each other and develop friendships.
4. Invest in the wellness of your staff. Promote healthy work habits, food choices, and emphasize exercise. Teach your employees coping mechanisms on how to recover from stress.
5. Streamline paperwork and administrative processes to make it easy for an employee to work, be paid, and update their information.
6. Consider what perks you offer your staff. Make them available to everyone but avoid thinking that that is all it takes to create a positive employee experience.

Notes

1. Jacob Morgan, "Why the Future of Work Is All about the Employee Experience," *Forbes*, May 27, 2015. http://www.forbes.com/sites/jacobmorgan/2015/05/27/why-the-future-of-work-is-all-about-the-employee-experience/
2. Immanuel Kant, *The Critique of Pure Reason*, trans. Norman Kemp Smith (New York, NY: St. Martin's Press, 1929, 1965), pp. 41-48.
3. Cited in Amy Morin, "How to Use Color Psychology to Give Your Business an Edge," *Forbes*, February 4, 2014. http://www.forbes.com/sites/amymorin/2014/02/04/how-to-use-color-psychology-to-give-your-business-an-edge
4. L. Edwards and P. Torcellini, *A Literature Review of the Effects of Natural Light on Building Occupants* (Golden, CO: National Renewable Energy Laboratory, 2002).
5. Bruce J. Avolio, Jane M. Howell, and John J. Sosik, "A Funny Thing Happened on the Way to the Bottom Line: Humor as a Moderator of Leadership Style Effects," *Academy of Management Journal* 42, no. 2 (1999): 219–227. doi: 10.2307/257094

6. "Ergonomics," Merriam-Webster.com. http://www.merriam-webster.com/dictionary/ergonomics

7. Quoted in Christina Binkley, "The Importance of Being Ergonomic: When Office Chairs Wreak Havoc," *Wall Street Journal*, June 11, 2009. http://blogs.wsj.com/juggle/2009/06/11/the-importance-of-being-ergonomic-when-sitting-at-a-desk-wreaks-havoc/

8. Bryan Hornik, "Know the Benefits of an Ergonomics Program," *Safety+Health*, May 22, 2016. http://www.safetyandhealthmagazine.com/articles/print/14079-know-the-benefits-of-an-ergonomics-program

9. Gallup, "Item 10: I Have a Best Friend at Work," *Business Journal*, May 26, 1999. http://www.gallup.com/businessjournal/511/item-10-best-friend-work.aspx

10. *Culture Hacker* podcast, 2017. Season 1, Episode 3. On-air talent includes: Mark Sawyier, Shane Green.

11. CareerBuilder, "One-Third of Workers Say Office Temperature Affects Their Productivity, Finds New CareerBuilder Survey," *PR Newswire*, December 15, 2009. http://www.prnewswire.com/news-releases/one-third-of-workers-say-office-temperature-affects-their-productivity-finds-new-careerbuilder-survey-79296112.html

12. Kate Harrison, "Best Practices for Setting Up Your Office to Maximize Employee Productivity," *Forbes*, June 25, 2015. http://www.forbes.com/sites/kateharrison/2015/06/25/a-new-infographic-offers-best-practices-for-setting-up-your-office-to-maximize-employee-productivity

13. Lisa Evans, "The Not So Silent Office Productivity Killer," *Fast Company*, November 17, 2014. https://www.fastcompany.com/3038590/secrets-of-the-most-productive-people/the-not-so-silent-office-productivity-killer

14. Greg Justice, "The Impact of Obamacare on Corporate Wellness Programs," *Corporate Wellness Magazine*, March 10, 2015. http://www.corporatewellnessmagazine.com/column/the-impact-of-obamacare-on-corporate-wellness-programs/

15. 24 Seven, *2016 Job Market Report*, n.d. https://cdn2.hubspot.net/hubfs/706318/Salary_Survey/Job_Market_Report_2016_resized.pdf?submissionGuid=da0ee869-cdbb-4b22-be98-bed44e50dfc6

16. Rebecca Greenfield, "How to Make Flexible Work Schedules a Reality," *Bloomberg*, January 21, 2016. https://www.bloomberg.com/news/articles/2016-01-21/how-to-make-flexible-work-schedules-a-reality

17. Kevin Kruse, "Top 10 Benefits of Working from Home (Survey Results)," *Forbes*, December 18, 2012. http://www.forbes.com/sites/kevinkruse/2012/12/18/benefits-working-from-home/

18. Laszlo Bock, "Passion, Not Perks," *Think with Google* (September 2011). https://www.thinkwithgoogle.com/articles/passion-not-perks.html

19. Dropbox, "About Dropbox," n.d. https://www.dropbox.com/about

20. "2014 World's 50 Most Innovative Companies," *Fast Company* (February, 2014). https://www.fastcompany.com/most-innovative-companies/2014/dropbox

21. *ReferralCandy*, "Culture Is Built, Not Bought: 14 Examples of Great Company Culture." http://www.referralcandy.com/blog/company-culture-14-case-studies/

22. Dropbox, "Dropbox Paper," n.d. http://www.dropbox.com/paper

23. Dropbox, "Benefits and Perks," n.d. https://www.dropbox.com/jobs/perks

13

Leadership

Why We Have So Many Managers but So Few Leaders

If your actions inspire others to dream more, learn more, do more, and become more, you are a leader.

John Quincy Adams, U.S. President[1]

MANAGERS MORE THAN ANY OTHER cultural mechanism, influence how employees feel about coming to work and what they do. When managers are able to inspire their employees to perform at a higher level, to stay longer, and to take care of their customers better, they exhibit leadership—our final cultural mechanism.

You could argue, and I would agree, that everything we have discussed so far is about leadership. After all, I believe great managers focus on how to deliver results through maximizing the talents, abilities, and strengths of their people. They do this by employing, leveraging, and focusing in on many of the mechanisms we have discussed, such as hiring the right people, onboarding them, enabling and empowering their performance, recognizing results, having tough conversations, communicating effectively, and focusing on career development.

While other chapters in this book have discussed a number of things managers can do to positively influence employees' attitudes and mindsets or be better leaders, this chapter reminds all managers how they inspire their people not by what they do, but by who they are. Although any manager can utilize and leverage the mechanisms described in this book, I believe that leaders have a little something more that makes others *want* to work hard and excel for them. And it all starts with the manager's own attitude.

Never forget that one of the biggest influences on the attitude of each and every employee within your company is the attitude of their direct manager. If the manager is not positive, how can we expect anything different from the staff? I recognize that managers are not always going to be on—they are, after all, only human. But what about those managers in key positions who always seem to be off? They are not passionate about what they do, they don't put in the required effort or continue to learn and grow as they should, and they don't care enough for those they are responsible for. As you think about yourself or your own management team, consider each person's capacity to positively influence the mindset of their staff.

The old saying that people don't leave jobs, they leave managers is still very true today and something we can never forget. According to Craig Cochran in his book *Becoming a Customer-Focused Organization*, "Management has the single biggest effect on [the] organizational environment, which means it also has the single biggest effect on attitude. Bad attitude equals poor leadership."[2]

Now is a good time to explain that I define "management" and "leadership" differently. Management is about the hard skills required to run a business, perform a task, or get work done. It is about planning, organizing, and doing things right. Leadership, in contrast, involves softer skills that focus more on how to maximize employees' abilities and performance through inspiration and development. You need both in your organization, and as John Kotter suggested in his renowned *Harvard Business Review* article, "What Leaders Really Do": "The real challenge is to combine strong leadership and strong management and use each to balance the other."[3] Leadership and management are not the same thing, but they are both necessary to the success of the organization.

Now, the way we normally acquire managers is by promoting employees who are the best at completing a task or have a certain expertise; however, this does not necessarily mean they are best suited to inspire or lead others. Although expertise is one of my key considerations for being able to inspire others, it is not enough on its own to make managers want to be there and want to do a great job. Unfortunately, this is why there are so many managers and so few leaders. While we continue to focus on promoting people into management positions for being the best at doing a job, companies often fail to consider a person's passion, effort, and capacity to care when deciding who should be responsible for other people.

I meet managers all the time who just shouldn't be responsible for other people—they do not have the capacity or in some cases the interest to lead so why not just leave them to what they are best at, completing tasks and keep the business going. They are necessary, but the problem arises when we give them responsibility for the employee experience, something they just do not have the disposition to positively shape.

After years of running and consulting for multiple companies, I discovered there is one idea that will always remain true when it comes to your staff. You cannot make them stay, make them perform at their best, or make them take care of your customers. They must want this for themselves. Organizations and managers influence this "want" by the experience they provide for their employees. We have covered the mechanisms that the organization is responsible for so far in this book so now let's talk specifically to the managers.

I think there are four key elements that are critical for a manager to possess that will help them inspire the right mindset and attitude in their people: passion, effort, expertise or experience, and caring. As you read this consider if your managers or you are fulfilling this critical leadership role.

Passion

As a manager, passion starts with loving the job. Employees are naturally attracted to those with passion, and that passion is contagious. Some managers lose their passion over the years, but many more just never had it; they have progressed in an industry, within a business, or at a job without really being excited about what they do or whom they do it for each day. Even worse, as they have found themselves in positions of authority, they have not embraced the possibility or responsibility of making a positive difference for others. As a result, they are unhappy at work, which leads their employees to feel the same.

Without passion, leaders cannot move others to *want* to do what they want them to do. Leadership author Robin Sharma wrote, "Influence is about spreading the passion you have for your work."[4] Passion is a requirement for all managers to have if they want to influence their people positively. Do you have managers who can excite others and share their love for what they do?

If you do not love what you do, be honest with yourself and consider a change. Life is way too short to be doing something you care little about. In one of my trips to New York, I met an Uber driver who had recently quit the Wall Street scene because he had lost his love for it. He was now working on his own business and reconnecting with his first love, art. He also told me he felt happy for the first time in a long time and that his wife and kids loved the rejuvenated him. Don't be afraid to follow your passions or help others to find theirs.

Effort

A manager must put in the effort every day. As Michael Jordan, the basketball great, said, "Sometimes, things may not go your way, but the effort should be there every single night."[5] For a manager, that effort needs to be there each and every day, but we have to be careful not to confuse being busy with being productive. As philosopher Henry David Thoreau said, "It is not enough to be busy. . . . The question is, what are we busy about?"[6] Are your managers focused on and engaged in doing the right stuff, especially when you consider all the mechanisms discussed in this book?

When it comes to effort, staff members need to see that effort in action, and it is best seen when it happens alongside staff members. Managers must be willing to get in and help, be there when it is busy, step in for the staff when customers do not play nice, or just show up and take care of things. When managers get into the operation or work alongside the staff, they can coach, communicate, lead by example, show off skills, and be calm when things go wrong, all of which ensure a level of respect from the team. This commitment to the people they work with elevates managers to leadership roles and allows them to inspire their team.

When it comes to effort you have to consider if your managers have the necessary energy to deliver on all their responsibilities. Tony Schwartz and Catherine McCarthy, executives at The Energy Project, a consulting group that transforms people and companies, define energy as "the capacity to work."[7] Over time, a manager's capacity to work can be severely impacted by stress, age, family, and a whole series of personal issues and ailments developed outside of work. Remember, there is a responsibility by every company to deliver an experience for your managers that sets them up to be successful and excellent at what they do. Ensure they get the inspiration, breaks, education, and support so that they have the mindset and capacity to perform in all that they do.

Expertise and Experience

Managers must have credibility as experts and have experience to inspire others to want to do well. They have to know what to do and have the confidence and credibility to share that with those they are responsible for. Knowing their stuff allows managers to excel in the coaching role and to better help their team perform at the highest level. As mountaineer Anatoli Boukreev said, "I offer my expertise and experience for hire in order to help a group of people reach the summit."[8] If we imagine that, for our employees, the summit is each of them achieving the highest level of potential at work, then it is a manager's expertise and experience that can inspire them to get there.

As experts, managers must be committed to learning and have a certain curiosity about how to improve. They look both inside and outside of their industry to see who is doing what, connect with other experts, and have a willingness to challenge the company's and their own way of doing things. Managers don't have to know it all to be experts, but they do have to be willing to find out who does know when they do not. I believe that learning is aligned closely with leadership, because once you think you know it all and stop growing, you can no longer influence growth in others. As David Mendlewicz, cofounder of Butterfly, a management coaching software company, wrote, "Management is an art that must be practiced and remembered day in and day out, and it's incumbent upon firms to realize this and implement the right tools for continuous learning and development."[9]

Caring

Finally, leaders must show that they care about their people. The only way to inspire teams is to care about them. The old saying "People don't care how much you know until they know how much you care" applies today more than ever. Show an interest in your people beyond the job they do. Respect them, which means recognize them and see what they do. Be approachable and available to the team as required. By caring for your people, you allow them to be comfortable and confident in their roles and their future with the company. As an ancient Chinese proverb says, "From caring comes courage." This courage is exactly what great leaders can give their teams.

In this chapter, rather than offer a case study, we have provided an example of a leader who we believe embodies the four characteristics of leadership and has made a difference to his company's culture by emphasizing employee experience.

Case Study: Howard Schultz's Leadership Style

Howard Schultz, former CEO and Executive Chairman of the Board of Starbucks, is undoubtedly a great example of leadership, encompassing the four attributes I have described. Not only is Starbucks a successful business with a world-class customer experience, but the Starbucks culture is also one that I have admired over the years. They have been ranked by Forbes, Fortune, and Glassdoor as a great place to work. Here is a part of Howard Schultz's story, to demonstrate his passion, effort, expertise and experience, and caring leadership style.

Passion:
"Howard Schultz has always wanted to do something bigger than selling caffeine," said Bryant Simon, author of *Everything but the Coffee*.[10] Schultz's vision was to create a place for human connection, conversation, and community, for his customers and partners alike. Schultz's passion for the business itself also showed through daily—he woke at 4 a.m. to study the previous day's sales reports. Per a Forbes interview, even the tiniest details worried him, because deep down he still thought of each store as *his* store.[10]

Effort:
Since taking charge of Starbucks, Schultz turned a regional company into a top brand worldwide. The awards he has received attest to the effort he put

into his company—Schultz was Fortune's 2011 Businessperson of the Year for delivering record financial returns, and all the while he was putting in the effort to spur job creation in struggling cities in the United States.[11] He has also been honored with various leadership and business ethics awards.

Expertise and Experience:

Howard Schultz didn't start out as an expert in the coffee or business world, but he chose to surround himself by experts. After the company's struggles in the mid 2000s, Schultz "beefed up Starbucks' management team with a wide range of proven leaders from outside. . . . The payoff: growth that never stops."[12] He dedicated his life to his business and to learning from his mistakes. In his own words, "What leadership means is the courage it takes to talk about things that, in the past, perhaps we wouldn't have, because I'm not right all the time."[13]

Caring:

Besides its luxury coffee offerings, Starbucks is perhaps most well-known for its social programs and initiatives, both for Starbucks' partners and its customers. Schultz always worked to balance profit and benevolence, and his programs truly showed that side of him—to support military veterans and spouses, he opened several cafes just outside of military bases; he introduced an online college degree program for his partners; he recently expanded healthcare coverage; and he also partnered with other large companies to host giant job fairs in large cities, inviting out-of-work adults for job interviews.[14] Schultz's inspiration for these initiatives came from his childhood, when his father was injured on the job and was unable to receive any help. He said in a recent interview, "My greatest success has been that I got to build the kind of company my father never got to work for."[15] Schultz fully believes that he can bring good from his success. "We're not just here to raise the stock price. What can we do to use our strength for social good?"[16]

It is the combination of these four elements that I believe makes people *want* to fulfill the vision that Howard Schultz created—a place for human connection, conversation, and community. These leadership qualities will allow you to fulfill your vision through your people too.

Remember that a title does not make a person a leader; the person makes that title come to life with a combination of passion, effort, expertise, and caring. When these elements are brought together within a manager, they can inspire their team members to *want* to do what they want their teams to do. And remember, it is your managers who ultimately define and determine the mindset and attitude of everyone who works with them. As Kris Dunn, chief human resources officer (CHRO) at Kinetix said, "Culture isn't defined by most of us by what we see on the website. It's defined by the managers who are leading small teams."[17]

Culture Hack: Managers must inspire their people to *want* to do what managers want them to do.

1. Managers become leaders when they are able to inspire their people to want to do more, stay longer, and be better at all that they do.
2. Managers must demonstrate a passion for their company, products, and what they do.
3. Managers must continuously put in the effort to lead. Managers must be productive and not just busy.
4. Managers must have and share their expertise and experience with their team in order to elevate their performance.
5. Managers must show that they care about their staff by being respectful, available, approachable, and showing an interest in their people beyond just the work.

Notes

1. Ilya Pozin, "16 Leadership Quotes to Inspire You to Greatness," *Forbes*, April 10, 2014. http://www.forbes.com/sites/ilyapozin/2014/04/10/16-leadership-quotes-to-inspire-you-to-greatness

2. Craig Cochran, *Becoming a Customer-Focused Organization* (Chico, CA: Paton Press, 2006), p. 8.

3. John P. Kotter, "What Leaders Really Do," *Harvard Business Review* (December 2001). https://hbr.org/2001/12/what-leaders-really-do

4. Quoted in John Patrick Hickey, *Getting Personal: A Guide to Personal Development* (Carlsbad, CA: Motivational Press, 2016), Chapter 9, Section 3.

5. Quoted in Subramanyam Vijayanagaram, "Productivity Quotes," *LinkedIn Pulse*, August 9, 2016. https://www.linkedin.com/pulse/productivity-quotes-subramanyam-vijayanagaram

6. Quoted in Simon Reynolds, "Stop Working and Start Thinking," *Forbes*, July 18, 2011. http://www.forbes.com/sites/siimonreynolds/2011/07/18/stop-working-and-start-thinking

7. Tony Schwartz and Catherine McCarthy, "Manage Your Energy, Not Your Time," *Harvard Business Review* (October 2007). https://hbr.org/2007/10/manage-your-energy-not-your-time

8. Quoted in Rich Wagner, *The Expeditionary Man: The Adventure a Man Wants, the Leader His Family Needs* (New York, NY: HarperCollins, 2009), p. 66.

9. David Mendlewicz, email message to author, December 12, 2016.

10. George Anders, "Howard Schultz's Stormy Crusades: The Starbucks Boss Opens Up," *Forbes*, March 1, 2016. http://www.forbes.com/sites/georgeanders/2016/03/01/howard-schultzs-stormy-crusades-the-starbucks-boss-opens-up

11. Starbucks Newsroom, "Howard Schultz: Chairman and Chief Executive Officer," n.d. https://news.starbucks.com/leadership/howard-schultz

12. George Anders, "Howard Schultz's Stormy Crusades: The Starbucks Boss Opens Up."

13. Claire Cain Miller, "A Changed Starbucks. A Changed C.E.O.," *New York Times*, March 12, 2011. http://www.nytimes.com/2011/03/13/business/13coffee.html

14. Maggie McGrath, "Howard Schultz Stepping Down as Starbucks CEO," *Forbes*, December 1, 2016. http://www.forbes.com/sites/maggiemcgrath/2016/12/01/howard-schultz-stepping-down-as-starbucks-ceo

15. "Howard Schultz: Starbucks' First Mate," *Entrepreneur*, October 10, 2008. https://www.entrepreneur.com/article/197692

16. Maggie McGrath, "Howard Schultz Stepping Down as Starbucks CEO."

17. Kris Dunn, "Culture, Zappos and Drinking Games," *Workforce*, June 4, 2014. http://www.workforce.com/2014/06/04/culture-zappos-and-drinking-games/

Afterword

Change—It's Not Just Something Everyone Else Does

The only way to make sense of change is to plunge into it, move with it, and join the dance.

Alan Watts[1]

I want to come back to something that I discussed in the introduction, the concept behind our Culture Hacker initiative: change and, more specifically, your willingness to change after reading this book.

Regardless of whether you are an owner, an executive, a manager, or a human resources practitioner, if you have come to this point and have realized that the mindsets and attitudes of your people or culture are not the ones you want or need because the experience you are offering could be better, you need to start thinking about what to do next. But before you even consider that, begin by thinking about your own disposition toward making changes. To be a leader in this modern economy you must be willing to embrace and lead the change required to improve the experience of your employees. We have introduced or reviewed a number of ideas in this book that have been proven to positively reprogram the employee experience. The question now is: What are you going to do with these ideas and will you invest in improving the mindsets and attitudes of your people?

Over the years, I have been involved in a number of change initiatives to help companies and managers shift perspectives. I have identified four things that leaders must remember when thinking about becoming Culture Hackers within an organization:

The Four Elements for Successful Change

1. Recognize the need to make a change.
2. Challenge the status quo with new ideas.
3. Prioritize your activities.
4. Get things done.

Recognize the Need to Make a Change

As human resources (HR) expert Michelle Crosby said, "Coming to terms with the culture you have and the culture you want, and knowing there are actually things you can do to move your culture from one place to another is every leader's job."[2] A person must recognize the need to change and *want* to change before that change actually can take place. Go back and reread Chapter 1, which lays out the importance of culture and the need to make the employee experience one of the main focuses of your organization. The imperative to improve your employee experience is simple; if you do not do so, then your customers and your best employees will leave you. Both of these losses will significantly hurt your company financially, your reputation, and your brand.

By recognizing that the mindsets of your people and their experiences with you are not where they should be, you can understand the first thing that can lead to change—the need. Now, as we indicated in Chapter 1, culture is not just an HR thing, nor is it something that can be done by one person alone. If you need to get your owner, other executives, and managers on board, utilize the information in this book to get them involved. Even better, share a copy of the book with them. Get your senior team to buy into the idea that your company's employee experience needs to be improved.

Our group has conducted numerous culture assessments over the years to help organizations understand their need to change. What is always most interesting, but not surprising, is that when we deliver and discuss their results, the overwhelming response from owners, executives, and managers is that they knew they had to improve. However, it seems that even when we know we have to change, we still want to avoid it for as long as possible. One of the most influential things we do is present a series of quotes from employees collected during the interview process. These quotes about how they currently feel about the work they do and who they do it for often become the catalyst for action. Consider if you are hearing and considering the voice of your employee. I highly recommend engaging an independent group to help with your culture assessment, even if it's just to validate what you already know. It just seems that employees are willing to open up more to third party interviewers, and the results shared are more likely to be reviewed.

Challenge the Status Quo with New Ideas

You must be willing to challenge your current processes, thinking, and mechanisms around the employee experience. Most managers struggle to overcome the most dangerous words in business—"That's the way it has always been." In many instances, the mechanisms and processes in place have been maintained for years. As economist John Maynard Keynes wrote, "The difficulty lies, not so much in the new ideas, but in escaping from the old ones."[3]

I hope that we have provided you with enough good ideas to support your own Culture Hacking initiative to improve your employee experience. However, I urge you, do not to stop learning just with this book. Remain open to other experts your employees, and your peers when it comes to the employee experience so you can continue to gather new ideas and get creative in your own thinking.

I know the task of Culture Hacking seems daunting, but the alternative is worse. As American business author Tony Robbins said, "Stop being afraid of what could go wrong, and start being excited [about] what could go right."[4]

Prioritize Your Activities

First of all, recognize that you cannot do everything at once, even if a number of items need to be addressed. Remember, one of the most fundamental Culture Hacking philosophies is to make big changes quietly. You cannot be quiet when you are suddenly all over the place trying to change everything. It is better to focus on one or two priorities and complete them properly, rather than trying to do many things for results that are merely average.

I urge you to consider all 12 mechanisms described in this book and determine what your most important needs are. If you are not sure, then brainstorm with others on which of the 12 are most important for your organization. When we do our culture workshop and consider which mechanisms to prioritize we consider which are the easiest to implement, which are most important to the staff, and the dollars and resources currently available for improving the employee experience.

If you are still not sure then get your staff involved. As we discussed in earlier chapters, utilizing their ideas, energy, and efforts is a great way to make your cultural shift a reality.

However, even if it does not come up as the most important element in your employees' experience, I urge you to consider your values as the first priority. They influence so many of the other employee experience mechanisms we have discussed and, as I have described, they are the foundation of your culture. Even if you think your values are the right ideals on which your business should be based, consider whether they are clearly defined and have accompanying behaviors that are easily observed and measureable. If you are not sure, then ask your people, test them on it, and watch to see what is going on in your business. Be willing to challenge and think about your values first.

Once you have your priorities, establish an implementation or change plan, and set some due dates to get things done. As indicated in the beginning of this book, although you can reprogram the employee mindset and experience, doing so is not an easy, short-term initiative that can be made up along the way. So give yourself time, focusing on just one or two items at a time. Utilize the action plan template introduced in Chapter 7 to guide your activities and, most important, ensure there is an accountability to get things done.

Get Things Done

And so our final point is to get things done. Now that you have read and talked about what is covered in this book, you have to actually get things done. As entrepreneur Wayne Huizenga said, "Some people dream of success, while other people get up every morning and make it happen."[5] All too often we tell ourselves that we are going to change and get things done, but we end up getting sidetracked, too busy, or daunted by the enormity of the task. Then down the road, we look back and wish we'd done more. So create your Culture Hacker action plan with names and dates for who is doing what and when things are getting done. Remember to look for the easy wins, the low hanging fruit, the things that you are probably already doing that with a few changes would be done. Engage the people necessary to get things done and make sure they deliver. Remember: don't be another company or manager where often more is said than done. Get it done!

Your willingness to improve your employee experience, putting aside some of the things that you thought true in the past and adding things that need to be true in the future, is the key not only your future, but your organization's future. I believe we are in the employee experience economy, and as such, we have to respond to what our employees need and expect from us today and continue to make adjustments along with our ever-changing workforce. As Kevin Ricklefs, the senior vice president of talent management at CHG said, "Culture change is an evolution—a journey. Strive to run the company better year after year. It is a long-term approach."[6]

That's it. I know it seems like a lot, but when something as critical as culture needs to be addressed because your customer experience is struggling, the staff's effort and performance is not where you want them to be, and your turnover is too high, focusing on your employee experience is not an option. If you want better profits and productivity, then make the delivery of a great employee experience and better culture your main thing. Good luck and thank you again for taking the time to invest in yourself and your team.

Notes

1. Alan W. Watts, *The Wisdom of Insecurity* (New York, NY: Knopf Doubleday, 2011).

2. *Culture Hacker* podcast, 2017. Season 1, Episode 4. On-air talent includes: Michelle Crosby, Shane Green.

3. John Maynard Keynes, *The General Theory of Employment, Interest and Money* (London, UK: Palgrave Macmillan, 1936), preface.

4. Tony Robbins's Facebook page, February 16, 2016. https://www.facebook
   .com/TonyRobbins/posts/10153960777439060

5. Quoted in Steve Matthews and Nick Gilbert, "Profile: Wayne Huizenga:
   Fast-Forward to Domination," *Independent*, August 16, 1997. http://www
   .independent.co.uk/news/business/profile-wayne-huizenga-fast-forward-to-
   domination-1245892.html

6. *Culture Hacker* podcast, 2017. Season 1, Episode 6. On-air talent includes:
   Kevin Ricklefs, Shane Green.

Acknowledgments

I would like to acknowledge the amazing team of people that I work with every day who helped put this book together or supported them in this effort: Michael, Laura, Alex, Rachel, Dana, Thomas, and Randi. I would also like to acknowledge my mentors and advisors who over the years helped craft my Culture Hacker mentality and skill set: Mum, John Hay, Bill Branson, Sandy Kelton, and John Gengarella.

Index